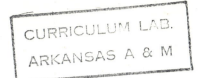

Teaching Reading Readiness to the Mentally Retarded

Teaching Reading Readiness to the Mentally Retarded

By

MIRIAM G. PIEQUET

Founder and Director
Laurel Learning Lab
Ontario, California

Publishers

T. S. DENISON & COMPANY, INC.

Minneapolis

T. S. DENISON & COMPANY, INC.

Standard Book Number: 513-01384-9
Printed in the United States of America
by The Brings Press
Copyright © MCMLXXV by T. S. Denison & Co., Inc.
Minneapolis, Minn. 55437

Contents

Chapter One
Introduction 7

Chapter Two
Sensory Perception With Visual Predominance 13

Recipes for Reading Readiness
(Visual Perception Games) 17
    No. 1—Pick Up Shapes 18
    No. 2—Shape-O 20
    No. 3—Shape Dominoes 25
    No. 4 26
    No. 5 26
    No. 6—Color Dominoes 28

Chapter Three
Beginning Letter Readiness 31

Chapter Four
Beginning Letter Readiness Continued 37

Chapter Five
Sensory Perception With Auditory Predominance 41

Chapter Six
More About Auditory Perception 47

Chapter Seven
Letter Formation 53

Chapter Eight
More Letter Formation 59

Chapter Nine
Capital Letters From Popsicle Sticks and Pipe Cleaners 67

Chapter Ten
More Sensory and Motor Development 73

Chapter Eleven
A Final Word: Love 77

CHAPTER 1

Introduction

Each child in your classroom reads a hundred things on the way to school every day. They are each reading your classroom now, and they are reading you. As Joey looks at the tables and chairs he decides which one he'd like to use. He has reacted to his schoolroom already. He has "read" it. He looks at you. Should he smile or scowl? He reads you and decides.

Since he is already "reading," your job is going to be easy. You have only to proceed as Rousseau suggested two hundred years ago when he stressed "gentle guidance of a child's unfolding powers" as the process of education. Gentle is the guidance you, Joey and Jane's teacher, will give as they plunge into the intricacies we call reading readiness.

You will know their physical and emotional needs as well as you know your own. You will make careful, fascinating plans to bring the world quite literally to their fingertips as you help them understand what they see, hear, touch. The first sweet taste of success will whet their appetites for more. You will be rewarded by what you will see. You will change their lives.

How? It's easy. Isn't everything that is fun much easier than if it is a chore? We have it on good authority that what Joey and Jane learn as fun is also what they learn more easily and more thoroughly. Good Dr. Samuel Johnson said as much when he pointed out that what a child learns *as a task* will do him little good.

So you and I will take laborious tasks out of school for Joey and Jane. We'll capture their interest with games that are not competitive frustrations. We'll watch them succeed, and we will reward them, not just for winning, or completing, but for trying.

We want each mentally retarded child to become a successful, happy citizen of the adult world. All of us learn better through concrete experiences, and as we learn to interpret them, the world about us takes on new meaning. So with the mentally retarded. We will teach Joey through concrete means and help him become aware of his sensory reactions to things, places, sights, sounds, smells.

To be a well-adjusted adult, Joey will have to be able to communicate. You will skillfully draw him out of his shell so he can speak readily and comfortably. Take his hand the first day he comes to school. Is it wet from anxiety? Don't let him sense your fear that you might not be able to "get through" to him. He needs your calm assurance. Take a deep breath and give him a smile and a sincere word of welcome. There is something about him you can praise. You've never met a child you didn't like. I know that's true or you wouldn't be a teacher in the first place. Jane may act very self-assured, and she may be. But on the off-chance that she is shaking inside, touch her hand and tell her something you find very pleasant about her.

See, you have already taken some giant steps to give Joey and Jane a successful readiness experience. This, from Robert Herrick, goes way back into the sixteenth century:

The readiness of doing, doth express
No other, but the doer's willingness.

So help your little "doers'" willingness to accept what you will offer them.

You will help your children to speak. You will help them to write, and you will help them to understand. Then later, when Jane and Joey build on what you have taught them, they can interpret what they have learned to read for information, for safety and, we hope, for pleasure.

Joey needs to be successful in order to have that important good self-image. He knows when he succeeds and when he fails. You will eliminate failure for him by being sure that each goal you set for him is one he can accomplish. If Joey is older than some of the others, don't let him think you are "watering down" his learning program. You can give him work involving the same principles you are giving Jane who is younger. But instead of sorting colors of yarn, he might like to sort the colors entwined in bits of discarded, intricate telephone wires. Instead of various-shaped buttons or beads, give him nuts and bolts and screws to sort, or models of road signs that come in circles, squares, rectangles and triangles.

But praise them both, young Jane and older Joey, and reward them tangibly for what they do. If you think a child's work is worthwhile and give him a reward that proves it, he will think it is worthwhile too, and then he is on his way. The reward cements the image of what he has learned in his mind. Bathe your children in success for things they do that are easy, in order to build up their confidence. Then they will put forth the effort to do something a little harder.

Oh, ho, you say. The reward is in the doing. Much later, maybe. Pleasing you will be a strong motivation, but a concretely rewarded response is the one remembered. Unrewarded, all Joey's interest in what you give him to do, and all the effort you put into making it interesting, will not hold it in his memory. What a waste, if it fades away as educators tell us it very likely will. So, do reward him. Give him a bit of nutritious food: a rai-

Bite-sized cellophane-wrapped rewards.

sin, a piece of popcorn, a bit of bite-size cereal, a tiny carrot stick. He could have come to school without breakfast. There is often coordination between the mentally retarded group and a nutritional need. So give him something to build his energy at the same time it builds his store of knowledge. But do give it immediately. If he has to wait till later in the day for his reward its effectiveness is lost. Do not confuse this with bribery.

8

Maybe Joey responds well to pretend money. Some teachers use tokens: white are a pretend 1c, red are 5c and blue 10c. With a wealth of such rewards over a period of time he can accumulate enough to "buy" a small car, a top, a flag, which he can keep. Maybe he'd like to buy some "free time" to listen to a favorite record, use the typewriter or play a special game.

As he grows in self-confidence, Joey can learn to take an occasional failure in his stride and know that some failures are part of life and not due to an inadequacy of his own.

Begin where he is, and let him advance in small steps. His instruction must be planned for him alone. If Joey already knows basic shapes and you need to present them to other students, he can do some experimenting with diamond shapes, hexagons, ovals. Let him use your templates of these, trace and cut out some figures, then share them with you and the class. Working on his own this way is surely a 10c reward job.

Do keep all your activities varied. Do not stop teaching a concept you think is learned until you know it is over-learned. Mentally retarded children often show a long-term memory equal to that of children without learning handicaps when over-learning takes place. Don't do this through infinite repetition, but do it through infinite variety. If it is shapes you are teaching, vary quiet, sitting-down lessons with some that let the children move about and talk. You can tape triangles and squares to the floor with masking tape in large move-about areas of your room. The children can "baby-step" around them (you know: the heel of one foot right up to the toe of the other), and trace around them with their hands. Try hopscotch in squares (the normal way)—in circles—in triangles. Don't make them try to jump it if they haven't learned to jump yet. They can walk all through the game for now, and hop it when hopping becomes easy, but do call it circle

Triangle Hop-Scotch.

hopscotch or triangle hopscotch so the names of the figures in it become familiar. You must point out the figures for him. Remember incidental learning is not the rule for mentally retarded children.

I hope you agree with me by now that the game is the thing. The child can evaluate himself easily if he wins or completes a game. Since it is a game, if he does not win he does not need to feel defeated. He knows right from the start that there is an element of chance in winning or losing, and this takes away his fear that he might be lacking in skill.

Your objective for a lesson may be such a simple one as having Allen tie his shoe by himself, or for Debbie to put away her materials. Allen and Debbie must know the objective you have in mind and you must motivate their desires to reach the goal and they must know that they can do so. You will lead each child from an immediate objective to your long-range goal by giving him new short-term objectives which in turn will extend a sequence of learning.

Careful sequencing is important so no child will be faced with a task beyond his ability. Every game, every exercise, no matter how unimportant it may seem, is evaluated by the child and by you and is rewarded so both of you immediately know when a skill needs further learning. This is when you will dig into your wizard's bag and pull out a new activity that will repeat the skill Mike needs but in a new and interesting way.

A game may be varied only slightly and present a new interest. If it is a Bingo-type game, just giving Betty a new card will sometimes give her a new interest; if it is a checker-type game, trading the color of checkers between her and her partner can give both of them a new interest.

Do keep a great variety of materials handy so you can invent a new game in a moment right at the time it is needed, but don't depend on inspiration of the moment. Most of your games will be very specially planned and carefully, neatly and artistically designed. These children cannot read between the lines. All material you prepare must be even more carefully done than for children with no learning handicap. Remember they think in specifics, and any deviation from the exact idea you want to catch their attention with may take all their attention from your main objective.

The objective of each game must be clear and specific. It may be a simple and immediate one, such as placing all the circles from a group of mixed shapes in one box, but your over-all planning including this game has a longer-range objective of discrimination of shapes. You are leading your children to the use of these shapes to identify letters and words, so you will take the child to an immediate concrete task one step closer to your long-range objective with each game. Any generalization you want learned will need to be pointed out by you. You always need to evaluate to be sure it has been learned. You must never assume that learning has taken place.

We want children in special education to learn independence and self-motivation. As Johnny repeats a learned activity several times alone he feels a growth in independence. He may want to mix all the shapes up again after he has sorted them, and separate the circles again. Let him do this if he wants to. Some inner satisfaction may be coming to him that is not evident to you. But do praise him for having done the task successfully several times, and offer him another interesting task. A certain amount of repetition of an activity contributes to the overlearning which helps him remember a concept, but he needs to be able to adapt to changing life situations. The child should be encouraged to talk about himself, even to vent his frustrations, and still understand that you are really interested in him. He will be eager to attack new problems when he remembers that you praised him the last time he tried something new.

Retarded children may not reach the reading readiness stage until they are eight or nine years old, or later, so the prereadiness or readiness activities you prepare for them will spread over the first several years of school. These older children will have a later start in their reading activities and therefore a shorter time in school to learn all they need to know as adults. So every minute they spend in school must count. Your sequencing of their learning must be much more carefully planned than for faster learners. One activity must provide the background needed for the next. You must show them the relationship between one activity and the next.

You will need an individually-written, detailed lesson plan for each child. The usual lesson-plan book can be used for an over-all plan for your class for each week. But, do rule off a piece of 12″ x 18″ manila paper with a space of about 2″ x 6″ for each child, so you can write in detail exactly what you have in store for his day.

No matter how carefully planned the lessons are, however, (here we go again—variety) be willing to modify them and build on spontaneous interest of the class. Suppose Jane brings in the brand new baby octopus her father helped her capture at the beach. Don't just say, "That's very nice, Jane," and put it on the shelf. Everything had better stop except octopus-type activity until the excitement has quieted a little. Then order can be restored if the teacher uses the octopus as a learning situation—learning about octopi in general and the care and feeding of this one in particular. When your children are satisfied with discussion of the interesting situation, they will be willing to go back to their more usual activities.

To record all the information you will be gaining about each child, I suggest a loose-leaf binder of a small size, perhaps 6″ x 10″ with a section divider for each child. Keep this close to you at all times for constant referral and additions. A few words jotted down in a busy time can be turned into a pen sketch later, but the idea you want to remember about Ann or Al will be preserved. These brilliant thoughts have a way of flitting away if they are not pinned (or should I say penned) down immediately. Pen sketches will help you plan exactly what Ann or Al needs to learn next and will save you having to rack your brain for that thought you really wanted to bring out at a parent conference.

I hope it is your school's policy to encourage parent participation. Remember you are only borrowing their children and parents are vitally interested in the whys and wherefores of your program at school. You should keep a shelf of books, pamphlets and magazines to check out to interested parents. Do visit the homes of your children. Parents usually are honored to have you come to see them, and you will get so much insight into ways of helping your children. Maybe Annabelle is over-protected in an affluent home. You didn't realize that she needs to be helped to develop more self-reliance. Maybe her home is a poverty one—maybe she has little to eat and little love. If you know she needs both, you can help. Through parent meetings at the school, as you explain the wonderful things you do each day, some parents may for the first time face the fact that their child needs special help.

CHAPTER 2

Sensory Perception With Visual Predominance

Johnny may be able to see, hear, touch, smell and taste quite efficiently, but be completely thwarted in interpreting the images these delightful sensory perceptions can bring him. However, skills of interpreting can be developed for him through your careful training. We often assume that a child understands a concept when he really does not. He may lack the background of experience to give the concept meaning. Your "gentle guidance" will bring this understanding to him.

Now this sounds like something too basic to mention, but surprisingly enough it's often met. Before a child can be assumed to understand pictures he needs to learn that they represent objects. You are now the producer, director and star in a demonstration of how we

Match the real object with its picture.

Match a manikin head to a real head.

Match the object to its beginning letter (sound).

can match a store-window manikin with living and breathing you, a toy dog to a real dog you bring to school for the day, a doll with Jane or Jimmy in your room. Then the scene changes. You show how you can match tiny reproductions of familiar things with real things: toy furniture with real furniture, a toy phone with a real phone, very small dolls or cars with real ones.

Finally comes the exciting day when you bring your Polaroid camera and everyone in the class can match a picture of himself to himself. Then, too, you will take a picture of the desks and chairs in the room and each child can orient himself to the fact that "this is my desk," "there is the clock," ". . . the calendar."

An enlargement of a picture of your classroom, mounted and cut so that each puzzle piece is of a whole object will help in the visualization process and give satisfying fun to every child. Don't stop yet. Make a puzzle of an enlarged child figure, mount it on cardboard and cut it, and have the children put the pieces together.

By this time the picture concept is very clear. Paste pictures of objects that go together on small cards so that the cards may be picked up in matching pairs: paper and pencil, ball and bat, cup and saucer. Let the children take turns picking up pairs of pictures, and encourage them to name the objects as they pick them up. Give them free rein to sort a stack of pictures from your picture file according to animals, people, houses, food, cars. You will have to help them see that the car in the background of the picture is not really smaller than the car at the front of the picture. Perspective in pictures—large and small, far and near—may be hard for them to understand and need specific teaching.

Since a child's attention is more likely to be captured by a moving object than a still one, use this principle in demonstrations before your group. If the lesson is one of shapes,

Match the size of a real circle with its picture.

Put the little one into the next bigger doll until they are all inside of one.

a large block rotated in your hands will be much more interesting than a still one on a table. Turn it to illustrate the fact that it has equal sides whichever way it is turned. A balloon may show roundness when it seems to float as you handle it. Let the children hold

14

it and toss it and learn the feeling of its roundness. Let them feel the difference in weight of the balloon and a basketball, though both are round. Show them a tennis ball, and it is easy for them to see that its smallness does not change its roundness. Show them the even smaller roundness of a marble. Finally the roundness of a picture of a ball will be easily seen and you can teach the circle as a shape.

Have a box of circles ready, all of the same neutral color, but in two sizes, large and small. Let them see that some are big and some are small as you put the big circles in one pile and the small ones in another. Have enough of them so each child can take part. Remember, teach only one new point at a time, so save your beautiful lessons on color until size differences are clear.

Take each individual shape through the same procedure, one at a time, keeping them at first all in the same dull beige or misty gray. Get some circles, squares, oblongs and triangles of wood (unpainted). Is there a shop teacher handy? Identify the shapes individually, as: large and small circles; large and small squares, large and small oblongs, triangles. Let the children play with them, build with them, *feel* them, until you can evaluate each child's understanding of the visual and tactile likenesses and differences in the shapes. Reward each child's success as he identifies the shapes instantly with a raisin, a bit of cereal, a cracker or a word of sincere praise.

Now you are ready for color. Use basic bright red, blue, yellow and green. Get out the squares of colored construction paper, the circles, oblongs and triangles you cut until far into the night to have ready for this lesson. Have all the fun you want introducing these bright figures and letting your charges experiment with the colored shapes.

Much conversation should go on through these lessons. They must not grow tedious to the children. Every object in the room has a shape that you or they can point out for an illustration. There will be some silly talk if they are having the fun you want to encourage.

One pitfall you should keep in mind. There can be a tendency for a child, if he sees a red circle, to associate *red* with his concept of *circle*. Or, if he is handling shapes and all the squares are blue, he may assume that blue is a characteristic of a square. You can get out of this trap by giving him plastic spoons of two colors. He will recognize the shape *spoon* and learn to sort the blue spoons from the yellow ones and still see that they are spoons. Help him carry this knowledge over to sorting the red blocks from the blue blocks. Then he will never begin to think he is working with *reds* rather than with *blocks*.

He may recognize the name "green" or "square" before he can say the name spontaneously. He may be able to match all the shapes he has been taught before he can tell you the names of the shapes. Don't worry, just help him say the names.

There is overlapping of skills in almost every type of activity. Clay use is definitely a tactile and kinesthetic experience, but also a perceptual device. It even has a characteristic odor which your children will associate with the pleasure of using it. Help them notice this pleasant smell.

We are starting a pioneering journey now into uses for all the knowledge your children have absorbed about shapes. We are leading up to development of letters. What are our letters anyway but a series of geometric shapes?

We will use our ally, clay. Help each child make a ball by rolling the clay on his table or between his hands. Let him enjoy seeing that he has made a ball or a balloon. Direct him as he flattens it and it becomes a pancake or a pretend cookie. Let him roll the ball into a pencil shape and it is a straight line, or a log to build a house or a part of a fence. He is really being creative, and loving it. When he makes several pencil shapes he can lay them in the form of a square, or an oblong, or a triangle. The large pictures of shapes you put at the front of the room will help him remember how these figures look. Perhaps you labeled them with the names of the shapes, not because you thought the children should learn the names at this time, but to help them know that letters and words that are printed have meaning.

A straight line may be a telephone pole, a broomstick, in a vertical position; it may be a railroad track, a telephone wire as seen when one stands out on the sidewalk, in a horizontal position. A circle may be a plate, a tire, a wheel. A triangle may be a tree, a scarf, a sail. Let the clay play be satisfying for each child before you take it away.

If you are a "ham" (most teachers are, at least a little) you can make a dramatic event of the dittoed sheet you will now give each child on which he can identify shapes. Do encourage conversation about the figures. Hold up objects or very simple large pictures of objects and point out the roundness, the squareness, the straight lines on the objects and on the shapes on their papers.

Your ditto sheet might look like this:

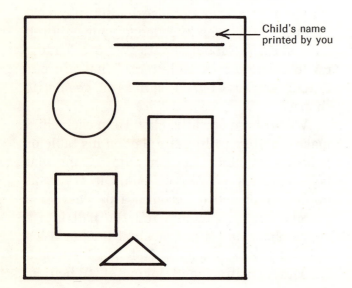

Child's name printed by you

You may want to use this paper for a lesson in color also and have them use their crayons. But this lesson also must be a directed one if it is to be of meaning to the children, so do direct them to choose the blue crayon, and check to be sure they have identified it, to color, say: the circle blue, the straight line black, the square red, the rectangle yellow and the triangle green. Any order of color for any shape is fine, whichever you prefer. The point is that the children need to know which shape is being colored which color; otherwise the paper will become simply busy-work, and these children do not have time for that. As they finish, present some reward immediately. The chart you have put on the wall similar to the one which follows may be the reward in this case as you put a star or a figure of some sort by each child's name. Remember, everybody wins.

SHAPES WE MAKE								
	Clay	Paper		Letter / Picture		i	(Pictures)	
Mary								
Joe								
Jim								
Ann								

This evaluation chart will be used for the next several exercises.

You may want to make templates from cardboard and allow children who still have difficulty with shapes to trace the templates with their fingers. Making the shapes on the sand table or in a box filled with moist sand will give a similar experience.

The following pages in this chapter contain some of my favorite recipes for games to improve visual perception.

Recipes for Reading Readiness

Visual Perception Games

Visual Perception Game No. 1

PICK UP SHAPES

Ingredients:

Copies of following page of shapes, mounted on tagboard and cut into 2″ squares.

Procedure:

Two-inch square cards mounted on tagboard illustrated as shown, and cut out, may be laid on a table, face up. Children take turns picking up a pair of circles, a pair of triangles, squares or oblongs. This simple game can be played in several different stages: first, the figures should be either without color or all black; next all of one shape may be of one color; finally the different sizes of the various shapes can be of assorted colors.

A final step may be added as other shapes are studied, and cards of different shapes made: ovals, hearts, diamonds, crosses. These should be made of different sizes also, and go through the stages of adding color after the shapes are well learned.

PICK UP SHAPES

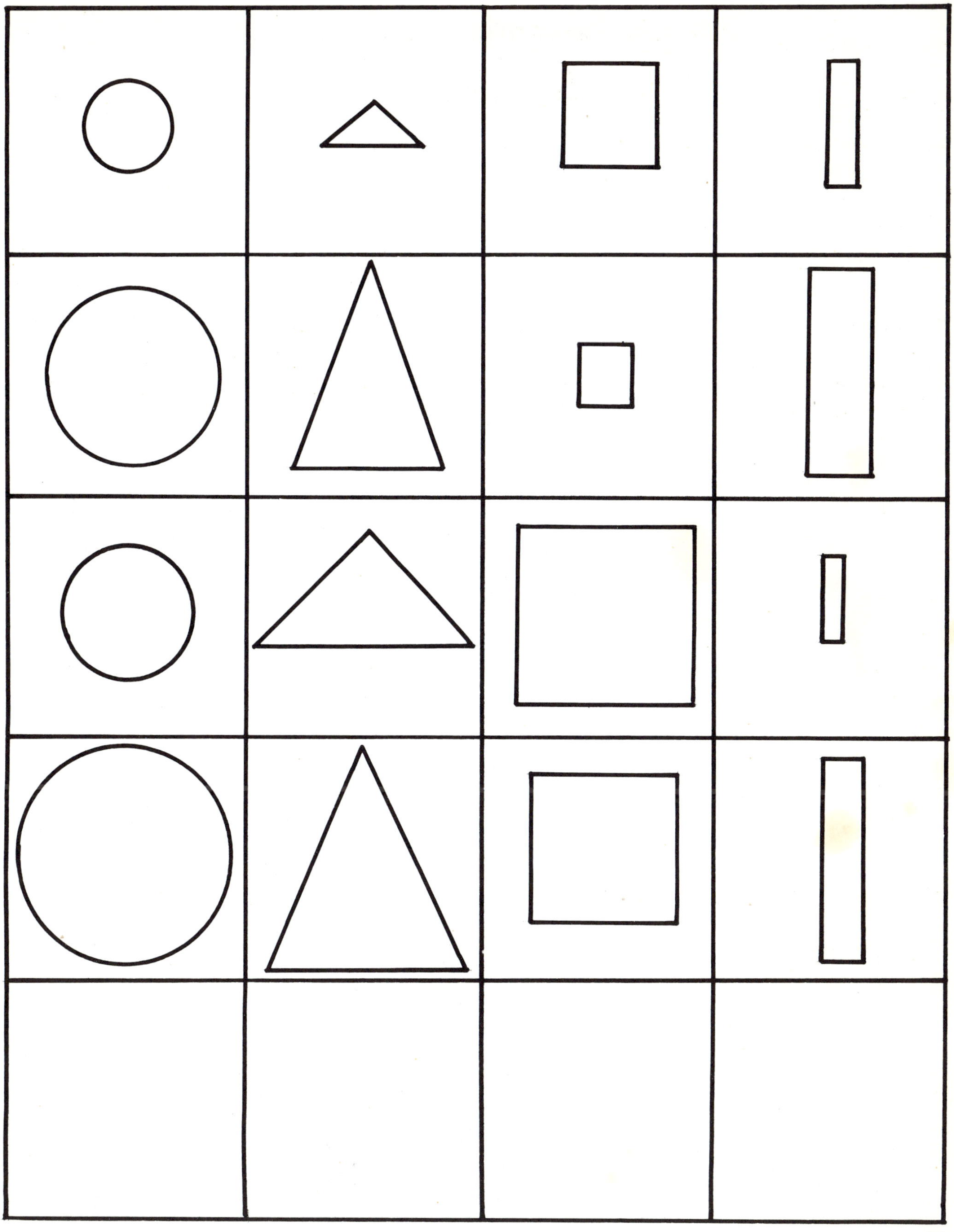

Visual Perception Game No. 2
SHAPE-O

Ingredients:

4 Ditto sheets (cards No. 1, 2, 3, 4)

Tagboard to mount cards (two of each if you wish)

Tagboard to cut 36 (or more) 2″ x 2″ plain cover cards

Procedure:

Caller will call one of the shapes and children will place a plain card over the correct shape. The one who has three of one shape covered first is the winner.

As with the other games in this series, a more advanced set of cards may be made with each shape colored a different color; then still more advanced with shapes of assorted colors.

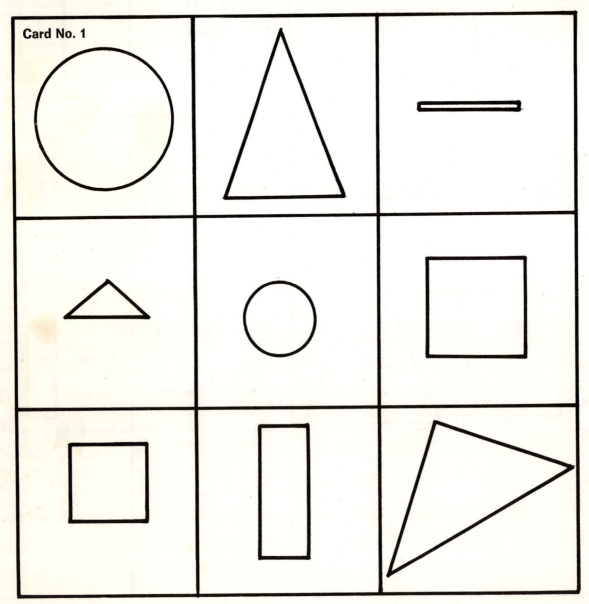

Card No. 1

Card No. 2

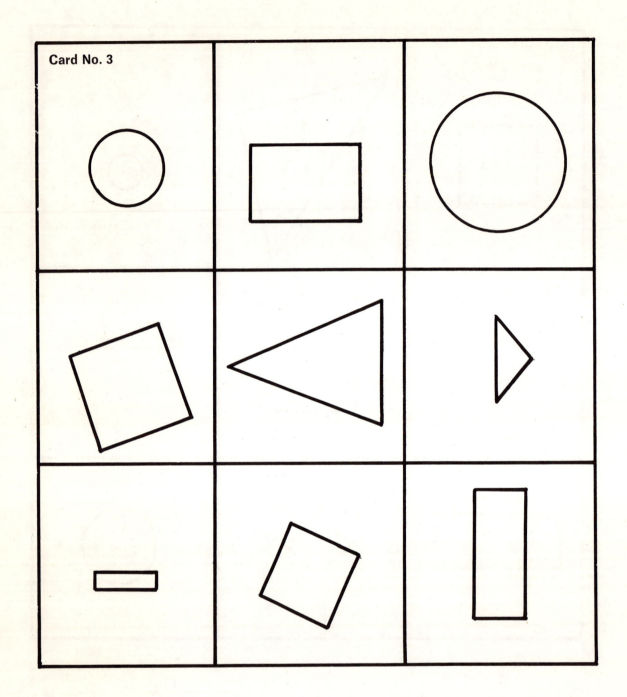

Card No. 3

Card No. 4

23

Visual Perception Game No. 3

SHAPE DOMINOES

Ingredients:

One copy of domino sheet as shown on following page

Tagboard to mount the dominoes

Procedure:

Each player starts with two dominoes and the rest of them are in a pile. The one who has a double may begin by laying it on the table. The next player may take a domino from the pile and if he has a matching shape, he adds it beside the shape that appears on the table. If a double is played, it is put sideways. Play can continue on any matching shape until one player has no more dominoes in his hand.

A more advanced game will add a second set of dominoes just like the first set, but with each shape of a different color.

A still more advanced game would be to make two sets like the first one, with shapes of assorted colors.

Shape Dominoes.

Visual Perception Game No. 4

Ingredients: (for six players)

Squares of colored paper 2″ x 2″ of red, green, blue, yellow, black, white; one of each color pasted onto a piece of tagboard about 6″ x 8″. Six similar cards should be made with the colors in different positions.

Squares of 2″ x 2″ manila drawing paper, enough to allow each child to lay one over the color on his card as the color name is called.

Procedure:

Teacher calls the name of the color and the child who points to that color on his card first and names it correctly lays a manila square over the square on his card. The one who has all of his color squares covered first wins. The children should add verbalization to this game by saying, "I have a *(red)* square." This may be played as an experience game and not as a game of winning by being the first to cover his colors.

Visual Perception Game No. 5

Ingredients:

Same large cards as for Game 4

Manila cards with the names of the colors printed on them, similar to the ones shown around the edge of the next page. One set for each child playing.

Procedure:

Teacher holds up a color and the child chooses the name of the color to lay on the colored square.

red

blue

yellow

(blue)

(red)

(white)

(green)

(yellow)

(black)

white

green

black

Visual Perception Game No. 6

COLOR DOMINOES

Ingredients:

The color dominoes on the next two pages may be made by mounting the oblong shapes on tagboard. The teacher may find it easier to paint the domino ends the correct colors and add a black line across the middle rather than by mounting small squares of colored paper.

Procedure:

The game is played similarly to the shape domino game. As more colors are learned, another set of domino shapes may be made, and a third set may include all of the color dominoes and a group of children may play at one time.

yellow / blue	yellow / green	yellow / white	yellow / black	white / white
white / red	white / blue	white / green	white / yellow	white / black
black / black	black / red	black / blue	black / green	black / yellow
black / white				

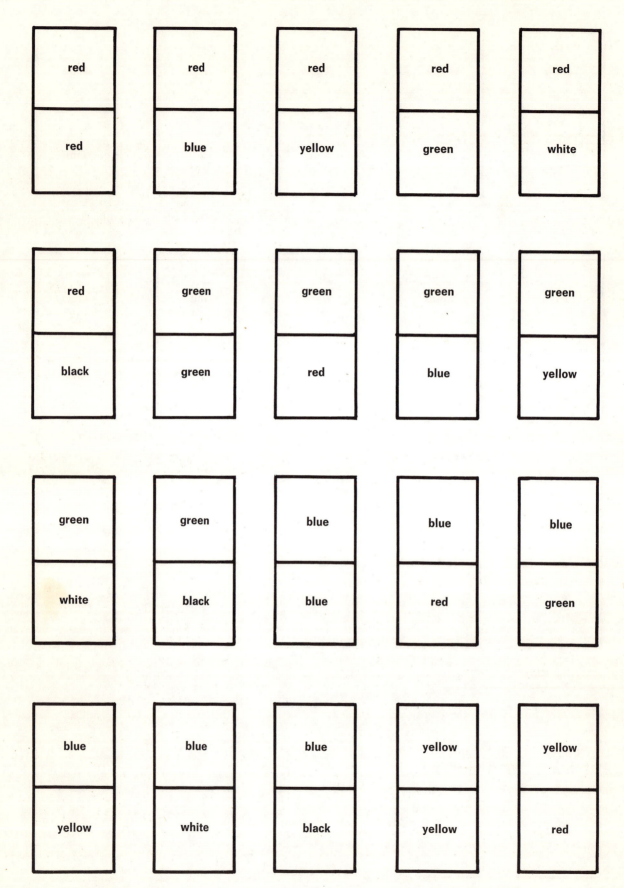

CHAPTER 3

Beginning Letter Readiness

Let's begin the letter concept with a review, and conform to the very best of techniques for every lesson plan. Our review for this important series of lessons will involve the use of one of the clay figures the children have already made. We'll carry the study of shapes into beginning letter formation and recognition. Quite naturally, at the same time we will introduce some beginning sounds.

But . . . time out for a few words of explanation about the Letter Line and Number Line I will be referring to. The Letter Line is your own individualized replacement for the alphabet line most schoolrooms have above their chalkboards. Yours will be a set of blank sheets (any one color which will suit your decorating plan) of 9″ x 9″ construction paper. You will be placing letters cut from black construction paper, one by one on the line as the lessons progress. Look ahead a few pages to the figure showing how your Letter Line will look soon. You will also see a sketch of the Number Line you will be starting.

Remind the children of the clay shape they made in the form of a pencil, which they called the "straight-line shape." Draw a heavy straight line vertically on the chalkboard and point out that this is the shape of a pencil. Tell the children that it is also a letter of the alphabet. Show the large cut-out you made of black construction paper and give the figure its name of "l" (el) and paste it on the Letter Line at the front of the room in the space reserved for "l."

Now comes a distinction you will need to make very clear. Many children become confused between the names of letters and the

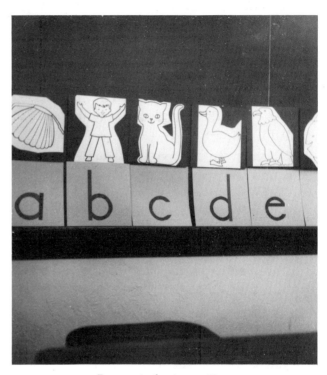

Fragment of a Letter Line.

sounds of the letters. As you know there is often little apparent relation between them: take "w" for example. Its name is a far cry from the sound we hear at the beginning of *water*. Now I am well aware that isolation of sounds is frowned upon by many educators and I agree with them in part. But, an occasional lapse from this theory will, I assure you, save both you and your children from struggling over the confusion between letter names and letter sounds in words.

So do give the auditory symbol to the letter "l" and then say that it is heard at the beginning of words like *lamb*. Tell them that the sound is said by letting the tongue touch the roof of the mouth just in back of the teeth. Tell them it can be heard also at the beginning of other words like *lion* and lady. Put a large simple drawing of a lamb above the "l" in your Letter Line. Point out again that the letter's name is "el." Tell them that it is sometimes heard at the end of words like *all*, and in the middle of words like *Sally*. Have them say something like: "The name of the letter is 'el.' El says 'l-l' at the beginning of *lamb*." This will clarify the distinction between letter name and sound, and this same technique should be used as each letter is presented. After all of the children have practiced the name and the sound this way, praise and reward them.

Tell your children you will be filling in all the squares in your Letter Line as they learn new letters, and when it is all filled in it will be the alphabet. Show them that it will be read "from here to here" (demonstrate left to right).

Since left to right progression is so important to reading, let's stress it right now. An interesting way to present it follows. You may repeat this exercise frequently, using various picture stories. Cut out a series of pictures in sequence, the larger the pictures are, the better. Mount them on cardboard. Tape them together accordion style (see the figure in Chapter 6) so they will stand alone. A flashlight turned on to each picture in turn from left to right as you tell the story the pictures illustrate, will show this important progression. Be careful not to have backward movements of the flashlight as you are doing this. Be sure to *tell* the children that the pictures read from left to right and that this is the way we do all our reading.

On writing practice papers which you will be giving soon, rule a green line on the left-hand margin for "go" and a red line on the right-hand margin for "stop." If you do not have ruled primary paper, make a ditto stencil as follows for beginning writing practice. Tell the children that "l" is a tall letter and should be written from the top line to the bot-

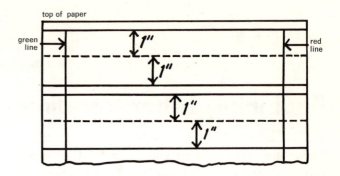

tom line, that the broken line they see is for shorter letters they will have soon.

You may use either a red and a green stencil, or a red and a green ditto pencil so you do not have to rule each paper separately. Be sure they know that the activity they are doing is writing. Oh, yes, a carrot stick is in the shape of "l"!

Match the numbered boxes to the picture of the number.

At an entirely different time, make an exact duplicate of the "l" shape you put on your Letter Line. Ask the children if they know another way we can use this shape to write something. If no one knows, tell them it is a "one," and paste your "one" on the first square of your Number Line. The Number Line should be on a different wall in the room than the Letter Line. Each child should have a Number Line of his own with his name on it, and on which you have placed broken lines in the shape of an "1" in the first block of it. Help him paste a "1" which you have cut out over the broken-line figure. These Number Lines will be added to from time to time and you should keep them except when they are being used. Don't forget a bit of praise or a more tangible reward when Jimmy has pasted his "1" on his Number Line and can identify it as "one."

The next lesson, built on the circle shape and leading to a new letter, will be given on another day. Show a large circle and have a review discussion of what objects have this shape. Put a series of dots (large enough for the children to see) on the chalkboard. Show how by starting at the top and drawing in the direction the hands of the clock go, you can connect the dots to form a circle like a large cookie. Then give the children a dittoed piece of paper on which dots are drawn, as yours were on the board, and help the children connect the dots with a red crayon to form a circle. Have them start at the biggest dot at the top of the page. You may have to help them find the big dot, and help them follow from dot to dot all around the paper until the crayon meets the large dot at the top again and a large round "cookie" circle is formed.

This is a complex task and many extra papers may be needed until a facsimile of a circle is made and when the task is accomplished a reward has been well earned. It turns into more fun now as the children may repeat the process with a blue crayon and then with a yellow, and a green. Each color should be suggested by you and identified so this is a color lesson. The circle can be traced with as many colors as you wish, until there

is a colorful circle outline picture. A suitable reward for this lesson is . . . guess what? Of course—a round cookie. This reward has historical approval as far back as before the time of Christ, when Horace, the Roman teacher, ordered cookies baked in the form of letters of the Roman alphabet. He gave them as rewards to children who learned to identify the letters. Be sure your children notice the roundness of the cookie, its fragrance, and its sweet taste.

In order to do the next circle lesson, scissors will be needed. If the skill of using them has not been taught, this would be a good time to do so. You should have both left and right-handed scissors available. Have you ever watched a left-handed child struggle to cut with right-handed scissors? It is more than little left-handed Cam should have to confront.

The procedure is simple and fun, but time consuming. Before using the scissors, have your children practice opening and closing their hands until an even rhythm of "open and shut" is developed. You will need several pairs of scissor-type kitchen tongs and let the children use these to try to pick up objects like balls of cotton or buttons or spools. When the time comes to distribute the scissors, you will need to instruct them to use their thumb and first finger correctly in holding them. They should practice opening and closing them before they actually cut anything. Now bring out a stack of old newspapers or magazines. Demonstrate making a circular "snake," by cutting about one inch from the edge of the paper and cutting around and around until you reach the center. Let them cut haphazardly at first, then let them try making a "snake."

Next give each child a picture from a newspaper or a magazine on which you have drawn a heavy black "frame" with a felt-point pen. Ask them to cut along the black frame. When cut out, the pictures may be pasted onto construction paper for display and reward.

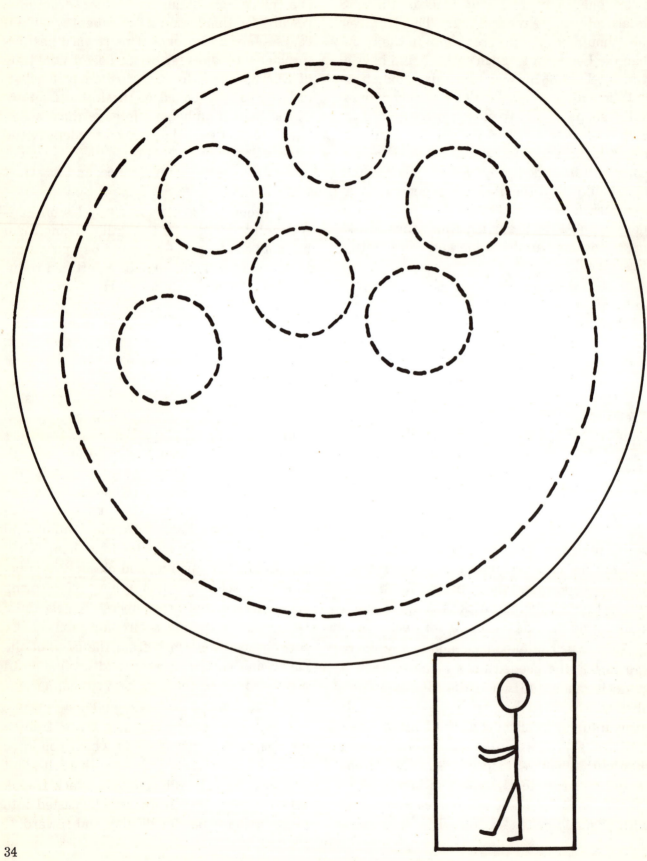

Now back to the circle lessons. A dittoed sheet like the one on page 34 should be ready for each child.

Do put each child's name on the back of the circle page, and do have some extra ones so no child will be left without one if his is spoiled. Directions are more complicated on this page, so take it slowly and easily. Remember how important the ability to follow directions is going to be all through life for your children, and don't forget "the willingness of your doers" is essential. The direction will be to cut around the heavy circle line, not the broken line. If you demonstrate first, and dramatically, it will be easier for them. When they have completed this, point out the broken line on the circle they have just cut. Have them start at the big dot at the top of the broken line and trace around the line with one finger. Then they may draw a circle by going over the broken line with a black crayon. The next step is to draw around each of the smaller circles, using a different colored crayon for each small circle. Bits of rewards may be needed between steps of this task since it is a little longer than the others have been. They are going to be very happy with the results though, so hold in there.

When the smaller circles are colored, admire the effect with them. Let them talk about what they have done. Next they get to cut out the oblong figure with the stick figure of a boy. Have them paste this on the lower portion of the circle picture.

Remind them of the straight lines they drew in the earlier lesson and ask them to draw a straight line all the way from each circle to the hand of the boy. When they finish they will be able to see a picture of a boy holding the strings of many colored balloons. There will be that intrinsic reward from seeing what they have made and that tangible one of the star you will place beside each name on the chart that was started with the clay figures.

A new day, and a new letter. Draw a large circle on the chalkboard and add a smaller circle within it. See if anyone visualizes the shape as a doughnut. Hold up the circle you have cut from black construction paper, with the center cut out to form an "o." If the conversation stays with the subject of doughnuts too long, you can divert it by passing out the cereal that comes in tiny doughnut shapes. Divert the conversation when you can with the fact that although the shape is a doughnut, the letter made in this shape is "o." As you paste your "o" on your Letter Line, explain that we hear the sound of this letter at the beginning of "oak tree." Show them that your lips form a circle when you say the letter and the sound "o" which is one of the sounds of this letter. Show them a picture of an oak tree; identify it for them. Run off some copies of your writing paper for a writing lesson on "o."

For another number lesson, choose a different day. Review the shape of "o" and tell the children that they can use this shape together with the number shape they learned as "one" to make a new number. Demonstrate by showing them that a figure of "1" followed by a figure of "0" makes the number they know as ten. Write these figures on the board. Illustrate the meaning of this number by showing ten small objects such as checkers. Show how a picture of ten may look like the figure below, just as the picture of one may look like this:

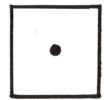 

Place black construction paper figures forming "10" on your Number Line and pictures of "one" and "ten," as above, over the numbers. The children's own Number Lines will need broken lines placed in the number space for "10" to show them where they are to paste the "1" and "0" you have cut out for them.

If you wish to take their thinking just a little farther, you may show them how two figures of "1" will form still another number which we call "eleven." If they remember this, fine, but there is no intent to teach the concept of eleven now.

Back to letters. Hold up a crayon and help the children draw comparisons between the length of the crayon and the length of a pencil. Help them speak about how much shorter the crayon is than the pencil. Remind them that the pencil shape became the line called "l" and tell them that the crayon shape will be a shorter line, and when we put a very small circle over it and call it a "dot" this shape makes a new letter "i." Back to black construction paper and a cut-out short line and dot to go on your Letter Line for "i." The visual and auditory clue for this letter is a picture of an eye so put one over the "i" in your Letter Line. Then hand out a piece of writing paper so the children can practice making "i."

A very short language experience story might develop after this series of lessons. The children will be anxious to verbalize about what they have done. Encourage discussion of the objects that were referred to as the line and circle shapes were made, and if you want to, sketch the objects instead of the names in the chalkboard experience story as you write it. Do keep it very brief and let each child who offers a thought for the story know which one of the words is the one he suggested. Later, in your preparation time, copy the story on tagboard and read it to, or with the children often.

Certain easy vocabulary words are almost certain to appear, such as:

we, a, red, made

Don't make them feel that you expect these words to be "learned" at this time. This is an introduction to the use of words in narration. You should point to the words as you read the story to the class. Little Tommy may be able to read it aloud, especially if he has had previous experience with written words. Let him have his day in the sun, even if he falters (you are always there to instantly help him). Maybe he only "thought" he could read it because he wanted to so much. Do be very careful that his all-important ego is not bruised by the fact that he couldn't. He deserves a very special reward for offering.

At this time your Letter Line and Number Line will look something like this:

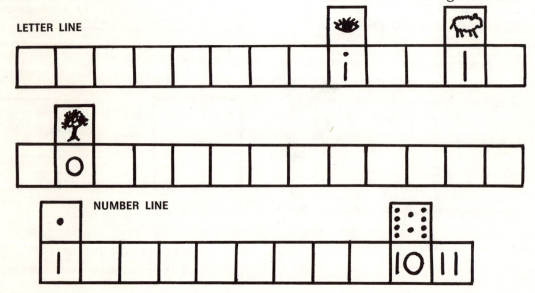

CHAPTER 4

Beginning Letter Readiness Continued

I'll present the next few lessons in outline form to save a few minutes of your busy time. The method is very similar to what was used in the last chapter.

First the oblong, or rectangle:

1. Draw a large rectangle on the board and lead a discussion of objects that have this shape: various boxes, a book, a crayon box.

2. Show the children that a piece of paper 8½" x 11" is already a rectangle shape. Give them a piece on which a broken line is drawn about one inch in from the edge and direct them to follow the broken line with a black crayon to make a new rectangle. The top line should be traced from left to right, then the bottom line from left to right. Then, if they turn the paper sideways, the two long side lines may also be traced from left to right. Have them cut around the rectangle they have drawn.

3. The paper should be folded in half where the broken line in the figure is marked, and then in half again, and one more time, so there are eight long divisions on it. Straight lines should be drawn from left to right with a black crayon on the creases the folds have made on the paper. When the paper is held so that the lines are vertical, the children will see a figure that looks like a box of crayons. When each section is colored a different color it will look like the crayons are in the box. If you have them do this slowly and carefully as a teacher-directed lesson, it can also become a lesson in color names as you direct the coloring of one rectangular "crayon" at a time.

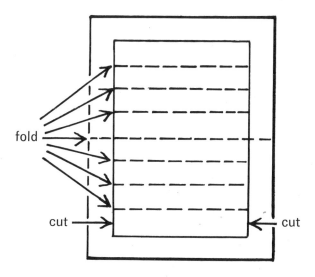

CRAYON BOX RECTANGLE FIGURE

Lessons on a square follow:

1. Draw a large square on the board and lead a discussion of objects of that shape. Demonstrate the shape with concrete objects.

2. Have the children trace around the broken lines of a large square on the dittoed paper you prepared, using the left-to-right method that was used in drawing a rectangle and following the line with a black crayon; cut out the square; fold it, this time in half one direction and in half again the other direction so that four squares are folded. With a black crayon have them mark over the creases, then using this new opportunity for a color-directed lesson, have them color each square with a different color.

3. The squares should then be cut out and pasted on a large piece of paper as blocks that may have been piled up by a child. The stick-figure picture of a child may then be given

to the children to paste on the lower part of the paper as if the child is piling up the blocks. If you have enlarged and made a stencil of the stick figure, the children can trace over the child figure with their black crayons.

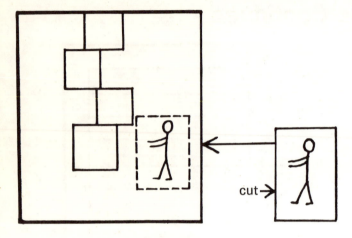

cut →

The lesson around a triangle will result in an interesting "Indian" lesson.

1. Demonstrate with a large triangle on the board, and lead discussion of what objects have this shape. Children follow dots on the dittoed paper you prepared to make a large triangle, using black crayon. Show them a triangle you cut from brown construction paper and explain that tepees, which are houses some Indians lived in, are made from animal skins that are this color, and that tepees look like the shape of a triangle.

2. Children cut out the large triangle from their paper and color it brown to make an Indian tepee. While you direct the coloring, show other pictures from your picture file of an Indian tepee. Each tepee should be pasted on a piece of blue construction paper (for sky) and the children should color the lower part of the paper green for grass.

3. You will have prepared another stencil, this time of the figure on page 39 of small triangles marked with broken lines for the children to trace around and color brown. Tell them the brown triangles look like tepees and form an Indian village. Have them color the

logs in the bonfire dark brown and the fire orange and yellow. If you have the children color the ground around the tepees green you are giving them a bonus concept of figure-ground awareness. You will know it, and I will know it, but don't tell them. Explain that the Indians used to gather around the fire in their village to cook their food or talk.

Triangles plus! Tell them that a triangle may be turned in every direction and still be a triangle (as on the Indian village paper). To illustrate this, and to carry the Indian motif one step farther, we may use two shapes together to form an arrow. Members of the class may be able to discover which two shapes we can use. A triangle will be the tip of the arrow and a straight line will be the shaft.

Prepare rectangles of brown construction paper, about ½" x 8" for the shaft of the arrow and a triangle of black construction paper of an appropriate size to be the tip. Small rectangles in different colors may be the feathers that direct the flight of the arrow. Give the children a blank piece of manila drawing paper to form their arrows and paste them on, to look like this:

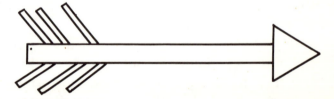

The children may want to identify the arrow shaft and the "feathers" as straight lines, which, of course, they are.

By now you are probably aware of many of the concepts that have been included in these lessons so far. To list some:

experiences with visual perception
auditory awareness
configuration
motor skills (cutting, pasting, folding, tracing)
hand-eye coordination

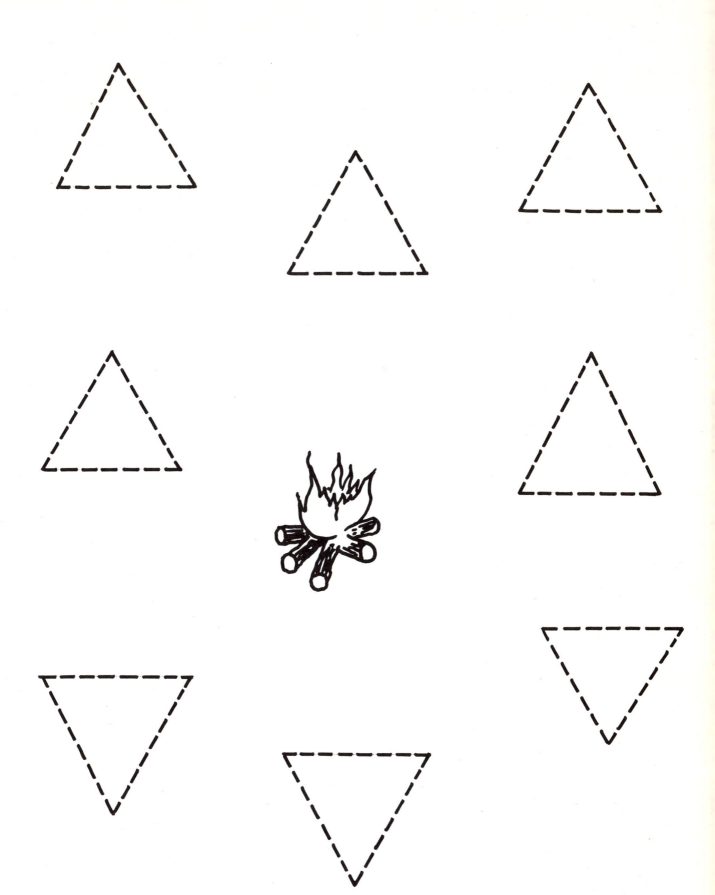

color awareness

shape awareness

beginning letter recognition

vocabulary development

picture identification

comprehension of spoken word

left to right directionality

identifying size

figure-ground discrimination

beginning awareness of numbers

association of letter symbol, sound and name

beginning story idea (language experience)

awareness of a few basic vocabulary reading words

awareness of "wholeness" in the Indian tepee picture

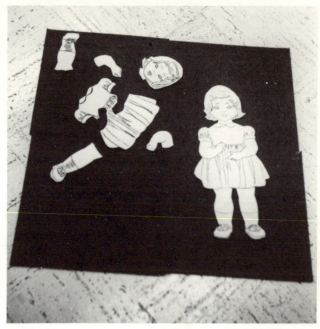

Put the doll puzzle pieces together into the doll figure you see on the right.

CHAPTER 5

Sensory Perception With Auditory Predominance

Listening to the speech around them is nothing new for Alexander or Patty. But do they listen with understanding? If you are going to guide them to the printed symbols we use for letters and words, you have to be certain that these symbols have meaning for them.

If Alex's hearing is impaired in any way he will not even be hearing the sounds clearly, so you must determine this first. How can he ever transform the sounds he hears in a distorted way into correctly spoken words, much less interpret those words?

You should suspect poor hearing if Alex often asks to have your words repeated, or if he seems to be straining to listen. If his hearing loss seems severe, do have him tested. Maybe he needs to be fitted with a hearing aid. In any event, whether the loss is severe or mild, Alex should be close to you whenever you are speaking. Don't expect him to hear you if he cannot see your face when you are speaking. He is probably learning to follow your lips, so do speak clearly. You should stand so that light from the windows or from the lighting fixture shines on your face.

Alex may be withdrawing and not participating with the others. Children with hearing difficulty often do this. Be sure you keep a cooperative attitude in the other children. If they tease Alex because of his poor hearing or speech, weeks of your careful work with him may be destroyed. Teach the other children to be helpful and understanding. If you use a little psychology on them, Alex may find himself overwhelmed with kind attention. Children are basically good, you know. You

may have saved him from struggling so hard he gets to the point of complete frustration, or from turning off sound entirely and withdrawing from talking. Some children do take the latter route. Then your work is really cut out for you. So do take an ounce of prevention for Alex's sake and for yours.

Learning to listen is hard for many mentally retarded children. Watch for those who confuse background sounds with those in the foreground, and try to help them hear the difference. These children may respond to a muffled sound of hammering down the hall instead of the sound you are projecting for their attention in the classroom. For them it is hard to focus on your voice in a background of normal classroom sounds. The problem becomes one of auditory figure-ground perception.

City children's lives are so full of background sounds that they often shut off all sound, as we feared Alex might. When this happens you need specifically to teach awareness of sound. You might start this way: have the children close their eyes while listening intently for any sounds that might be in the background such as people walking in the hall, children on the playground, the sound of a heater, or a bee buzzing.

Then make a series of sounds such as are often heard in a classroom. Since children may respond to different sounds before they may be able to attach names to them, teach the sounds. Illustrate them as you produce them, such as: tap a desk with a pencil, tap a chalkboard, close a book, tap the window, drop a coin, an eraser, strike a piano key, tap two sticks together, tap a triangle, crumple paper. Ask the children to close their eyes and call for volunteers to identify the sounds. Later two teams may be formed, with each team getting a point for a correct identification of a sound. Finally children may make their own sounds for their classmates to identify with their eyes shut. They may run, walk, stamp their feet, jump, clap hands.

As they advance in their auditory perception, they may copy a pattern of sound you may establish, such as: two short taps and two long taps, two soft taps and one long. They may do this as a group at first. Help them, and make a game of it. Then let individuals volunteer to do the tapping pattern. As in the other developments, the discrimination should be gross at first and less so after a time, sequencing the difficulty of the task.

There are records and tapes of groups of sounds, such as farm sounds, city sounds, things that go. If you do not have records or tapes available, make your own tapes of sounds around you. Tape them from radio or television programs; get your friends to help. Serve them a cup of coffee, and have a hilarious time. You can tape running water, a car starting, a jet plane, a dog barking, cats fighting, rattling keys, rain, wind, a whistle, siren, bell, clock, phone, door chime.

As sound discrimination develops, go into concepts of loud and soft. Project the sounds the children have already learned to identify by turning the volume of the record player or tape recorder to loud, then to soft, or alternate loud and soft sounds in the room. However, be sure the loud and soft sounds come from the same instrument, object, or animal for both loud and soft, to avoid confusion.

For more advanced listening, concepts of high tones and low tones may be taught. Silence is another concept children need to learn, and, oh, those blessed moments of silence.

Hearing incorrect speech patterns often causes what appear to be hearing deficiencies.

Even Dolores, whose hearing is not impaired, will need to develop auditory perception so she will hear sounds correctly and be able to fuse these sounds into words. Her parents speak another language at home and she tends to pronounce words the way she hears them. Then, words are pronounced differently by you, so she becomes confused. When the speech sounds she learns in school are related by you to the letters and words you are teaching, Dolores has trouble identifying them. Be sure she doesn't get the impression that what she hears at home is wrong. Just "gently guide" her so she can use both languages correctly.

Mentally retarded children frequently have inaccurate patterns of speech anyway, so an accent triples their problem. If there is no physical cause for inaccurate speech, try to encourage speech correction both for each child's social adjustment and for his progress toward a goal of readiness to read.

Here is a pompous sounding principle: in emphasizing speech sounds to a child with learning difficulty we should start with the general and proceed to the particular. For example, the sentence is a meaningful unit, so the attention of a child is more easily caught by a sentence or by listening to rhymes or stories. Stories that have much repetition in them such as The Three Bears, The Three Billy Goats Gruff or The House That Jack Built can hardly be improved upon. Even if the children have heard the stories many times before, presenting them in a new situation will appeal to them. These stories can be illustrated by teacher-made felt board figures. If felt is not available, you may cut out pictures and paste them on sandpaper to adhere to a flannel board. The board itself may be easily made by attaching ordinary flannel to a piece of a cardboard carton.

Tell the story rather than read it. After the story is familiar to the children they may want to tell it themselves using the flannel board pictures. The objective of this type of lesson is to gain the children's interest through listening and to encourage them to speak. These two skills are so closely related in preparation for reading that one can scarcely be taught without the other. The more verbal a child becomes, the more he grows interested in reading.

A few words such as titles for the stories may be printed and shown as part of the story. This is not to teach the words, but to acquaint the children that letters and words are symbols of speech. When the storytelling time is over, the pictures and title words may be kept where the children can observe them and handle them and become interested in placing them in story sequence as an independent activity.

Puppets made by you can serve as storytelling props, and are very helpful when opportunities are given for the children to tell the stories. Fear of speaking before the others can be overcome if a puppet is "doing the talking" for the child, especially if a cardboard screen made from a cut-apart carton serves as a puppet stage and allows timid Jim to hide behind it while his puppet is talking.

An improvised television screen also allows Phil or Cliff to feel unthreatened by his audience when he is speaking. This can be made by cutting an oblong hole in a large carton. If a carton like the ones used to pack appliances is used, this can double as a puppet stage. The carton can be painted by members of the class if you wish. Dials can be added in the form of pieces of the carton painted black, or wooden drawer knobs. The addition of canned milk to poster paint makes a shinier and more durable finish for painting a carton.

Why not start to tell a story and leave it unfinished, and ask for volunteers to answer "What happened next?" If the children hesitate to respond, an improvised "microphone" can be helpful. It can be made from a short piece of one-inch doweling with a long cord

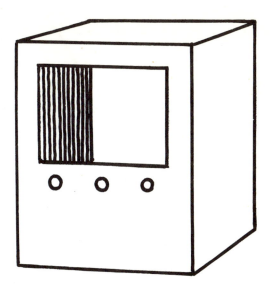

attached to it for the "wire." Or a food can attached to a piece of one-inch doweling and mounted on a piece of wood makes a very realistic microphone.

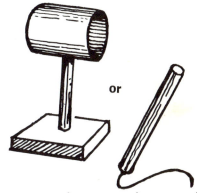

or

Other ways of encouraging speech include story starters like:

"What would happen if . . ."

"What would happen if I opened the window and a .... flew in?"

Providing further auditory and verbalization stimulation, say, "Let's think of all the things that can carry other things," or "Let's think of everything that has ears," or "Let's think of everything that has hair."

Or, ask: "Who am I talking about?" and describe a child in the room. The children should have their eyes closed and try to think which child matches the description.

Games like "Hot and Cold" will help chil-

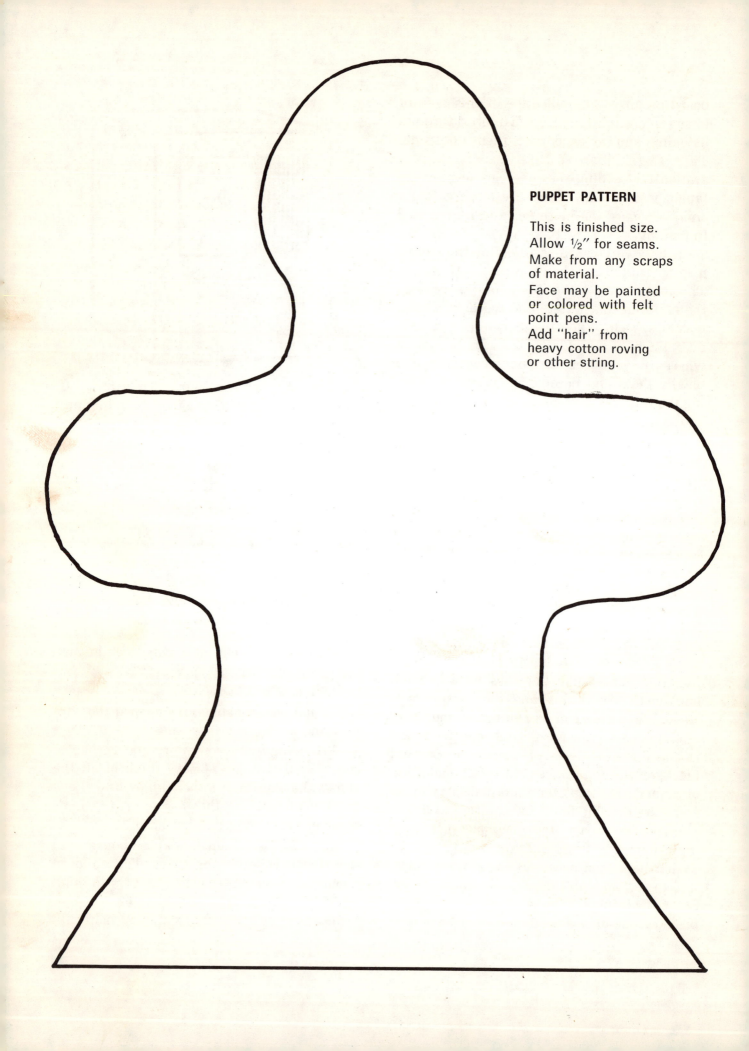

PUPPET PATTERN

This is finished size.
Allow ½″ for seams.
Make from any scraps of material.
Face may be painted or colored with felt point pens.
Add "hair" from heavy cotton roving or other string.

dren become freer about verbalizing, and will help the child who is "it" respond. Hide an object or picture and the children direct the child who is "it" to find it by saying "hot" if the child is getting close to the object and "cold" if he is going away from it. It should always be in an easy-to-find place, and you should give broad hints to help the child find it in order to keep him from becoming frustrated.

Simple riddles will stimulate many responses when you ask the questions.

What is all over a house? (roof)

What gets wetter the more it dries? (towel)

What has only one foot? (one leg)

What has a head like a cat but is not a cat? (kitten)

After verbalization has become easy for the group, direct their thoughts to individual words. Help them recall words that were used in the stories they have heard and the games they have played. An experience story about some favorite story or activity would be a useful activity now.

Certain words would almost certainly appear in the story:

| I | you | we | the | a |
| to | and | in | be | of |

These ten words make up twenty-five percent of all words found in ordinary writing. They should not be overstressed at this time, but can be carefully pointed out by you in the short experience story. It might develop in something of this manner:

_We_ had _a_ story about three bears. _A_ girl went _to_ _the_ house _and_ she went _in_ _and_ ate. _I_ was _the_ little bear. _I_ went _to_ _the_ woods. _I_ said, _you_ ate all _of_ my food.

Make flash cards of the underlined words, being sure to use capital letters where the words are capitalized in the story. Then ask Terry to take a flash card and try to find a word it matches in the story. Everyone will want a turn. By reading the story as many times as necessary, and having any child who wants to do so "read" it with the teacher's help, it will be possible for many of the words to be matched to those in the story. There should be no pressure in the activity, and no insistence that everyone should do this. The story should be attached to the wall or to a chart rack with the flash cards close to it, and it can be used as independent activity for any child who may want to try matching the words to the ones in the story without doing so before the class.

It enlivens a story for children who cannot yet read but are becoming interested in words to use a rebus technique in language experience stories. Figures like these may be used instead of the words and help the children feel that they are reading and add a great deal of interest. Sketch them in as you print the story, or have them ready to paste to the proper place in the story as you print it.

GOLDILOCKS
(the girl)

BEAR
(make three)
small, middle-sized, large

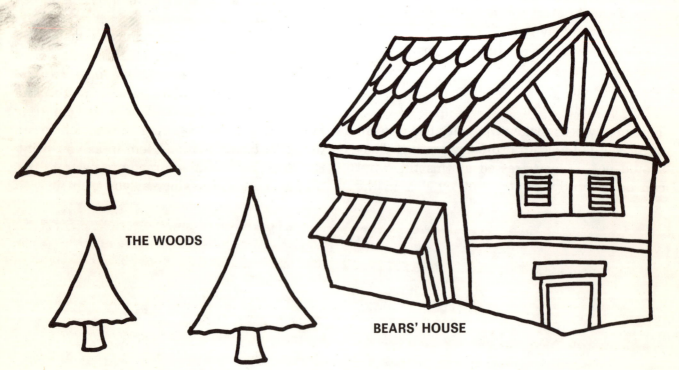

THE WOODS

BEARS' HOUSE

CHAPTER 6

More About Auditory Perception

The language experience story has led us to the next step in auditory awareness as we follow the sequence of general to the particular and go from sentences to the study of individual words. Since pictures are worth ten thousand words, let's start with them.

For Pick a Picture, you will need:

Four 9″ x 12″ tagboard or cardboard cards

Four large uncomplicated pictures

Glue

Masking tape

Directions:

Mount the pictures on the cards, attach the sides of the cards together and fold them accordion style so that they will stand on a table. Set them before your class, describe one of the pictures, and ask a volunteer to come up and point to the picture you have described. Then ask him to tell something about one of the other pictures, and choose a friend to point to the picture. If the first boy has received encouragement and a cracker or a raisin, enthusiasm will be enormous among the group to see who will be chosen next.

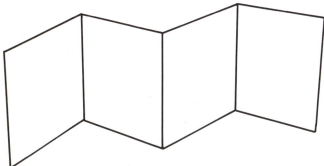

Since you have taught the children so much about how to listen, it will not be hard to teach them to listen for words that have parts that sound alike. They know the word "rhyme" because of the many rhymes they have heard you read to them and that they have acted out. You can remind them how Jack and *Jill* went up the *hill,* and Jack *Sprat* could eat no *fat,* and arouse their interest in finding other pairs of words. If you show them a picture of a lovely cat and a beautiful rat like the ones that follow, you may find "a-t" words like "fat," "sat," "mat" pouring out from your eager children faster than you can write them on the chalkboard. And write them you must, not that they will be "learned" at once, but memory of this fun time will be stored away and bring back happy overtones whenever the participants in the game look at the pictures where you have placed them on the game table. Starting with the lovely cat and rat, you should make another accordion display, this time of "at" words. After being on display for a few days, the accordion may rest on the game table to be colored as a "reward" by some lucky boy or girl who has earned a special recognition. Those not chosen to decorate the "at" folder will have their turns at coloring because you will be making so many such rhyming folders they will all have several chances.

If you find you suddenly can't even think of one word that would rhyme with "tack" or or "rug" or "dog" or "boat," run quickly to your public library for a rhyming dictionary, or pull out your handy desk one. I always try to have mine close by me.

Don't overlook language experience stories for each rhyming accordion folder you make. Of course, you must never let the children look on this as a task. Lead up to it by insert-

cat

48

rat

ing inviting little tidbits like, "I just thought of an exciting story we could tell about a cat and a rat. Did anyone else think of one? Oh, the rat really gets into trouble in my story!"

Using your accordion sound-alike folders as springboards, try saying three words from one of them and inserting a fourth word that is very different. Try "bell, well, tell, dish." Probably Jerry or Anna, always the first to catch on to a new game, will immediately hear the different sound and they will be thrilled to be the "teacher" and make up some more such sets of alike and different words. If others want a turn, by all means let them. Even if they cannot add a different word to three that sound alike they should get recognition and reward for being willing to try. Maybe on a second turn even Annabelle and Alex will be able to form a proper sequence of four. If not, never make them feel unsuccessful. They just need more audio-awareness. None of the activities in your room should be tests to see how well the children perform, but opportunities to see how eagerly they try.

Often you will find that auditory-handicapped children will form vocabularies almost entirely of nouns. So insert other words into your sound-alike games. Many words other than nouns lend themselves to illustration:

adjectives like *fat,* verbs like *float,* prepositions like *in.*

Don't forget round-robin games where Mary will say a word, the boy next to her will say one that sounds like it, the girl next to him will say another, and so on.

Please remember that the most important ingredient I can suggest for the recipe for a successful classroom for mentally retarded children is relaxation or freedom from strain. Not just for the children, but also for you. I don't suggest chaos, but freedom—controlled freedom. The kind of atmosphere that makes school the most wonderful experience in the lives of your children is what you want to establish for them.

It will be the most wonderful experience in your life, too, as you see what your understanding, empathy, and yes, love will do for them.

Never let little Leopold's belated response go unexpressed, even if it is time to put away the reading games and go full speed ahead into the intricacies of modern math. The math period will go much more smoothly if Leopold (who tends to be a cut-up) does not enter it feeling frustrated. Take a minute or two to let him give his response at his own academic rate.

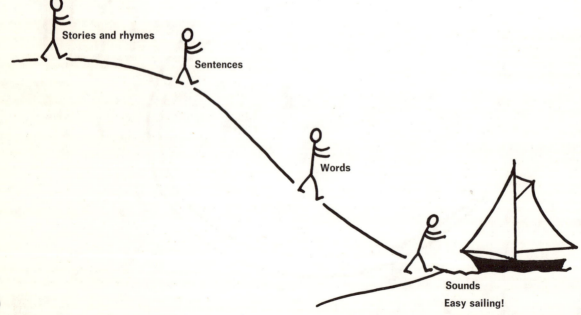

Stories and rhymes

Sentences

Words

Sounds

Easy sailing!

The academic word for it is retention, or audio-memory in this case if you like. But if you think of it in nostalgic terms of what memories mean to human beings, it becomes not so much an educational goal as a sanity saving experience. Remember the last time you went to introduce a friend and couldn't remember his name? Think how frustrating it is to forget and then have someone say, "But I just *told* you a minute ago!" It wouldn't help you remember your friend's name. And it won't help Joey remember even an important fact (important to you, but is it to him?).

Your friend's name flew back to you during a relaxed time when you were not thinking about it. So, we'll keep Joey's memory training time relaxed.

Recipe for Memories—

Ingredients:

A relaxed, comfortable environment
Expectation of pleasure

Method:

Guide gently into memory games.

Don't use "Simon says" until your children won't feel silly and ashamed if they respond wrong.

Do use a game of verbal commands and wait for each one to follow the direction.

Don't scowl or tap your foot while waiting.
Do smile and encourage each one to:

"Put your hand on the top of your head." (It can be right hand, or left hand, if they are ready for this.)

"Hold both hands in the air and wave to the people beside you."

"Pretend you are combing your hair."

"Pretend you are washing your hands."

Or, for individual responses:

"Go to the table, take a piece of paper, go back to your seat and crumple the paper into a ball."

"Go behind the teacher's desk, stoop down to the floor, then pop up like a Jack-in-the-box."

You can make up these directions by the dozens, but if you can't seem to think of any when you want them, have a list of them in your notebook or in your desk card file of ideas.

Don't hesitate to write down inspirations as they come to you.

Do file them as soon as written.

Don't lay the slips of paper under your desk blotter, or in the book you are reading.

Do put them where they can be found and used.

Try putting three objects on the table, then say:

"Show me the ...."

This should be worth a small marshmallow for quick energy. Or, if your dentist says "no," a tiny carrot stick will do nicely.

"Put your finger on the ...."

Another marshmallow or carrot stick.

"Give me the ...."

Another.

Put four or five different objects on your desk. Let the children look at them for a minute, then cover them with a sheet of paper and ask "Who can name the things you saw?" Add an object as the responses improve.

Say three numbers (then four, then five), and ask who can repeat the numbers.

Such little games can fit into those odd moments when tension may arise and in spite of your careful planning the lesson you allowed twelve minutes for is finished in eight, or when the milk is late in arriving, and though they seem pure fun to the children, are valuable learning aids.

Pictures, pictures to the rescue! Pull out of your file the memory pictures you prepared after school one day. You mounted them on the cover of a construction paper folder. They show some activity in which a number of people or animals are involved. You have written

51

six or eight questions about the picture on the inside of the folder. Now you can hold the picture before the class for a quiet minute or two and ask them to look at it carefully. Then ask question number one: "How many boys are in the picture?" (or cows, or clowns) "Where are the people?" "What color is the girl's dress?" "Is the horse standing or running?"

Similar pictures can go into a box on the game table for independent activity and one child may make up questions to ask another.

The play's the thing! So let the children put stories and poems they have heard read often into their own words and make spontaneous plays out of them. The costume box will have in it all the beautiful outcasts of clothing you can salvage from your closet or your friends' or from the nearest thrift store, the gaudier the better for bright moments of make-believe.

Or try a puppet play of Jack and the Beanstalk: the giant can let off a lot of steam by sounding really fierce as he says:

Fee, fie, foe, fum.

And so can the wicked witch in the Wizard of Oz.

Then don't forget the marvelously self-directive jump-rope games. Don't add the difficult skill of jumping rope—just use the verses for directions memory, but do let the children chant them as they do the actions.

A favorite is:

Teddy Bear, Teddy Bear turn around
Teddy Bear, Teddy Bear touch the ground
Teddy Bear, Teddy Bear lead the band
Teddy Bear, Teddy Bear wave your hand
Teddy Bear, Teddy Bear reach the sky
Teddy Bear, Teddy Bear throw a kiss good-by
Teddy Bear, Teddy Bear climb the stairs
Teddy Bear, Teddy Bear say your prayers.

You will find a tremendous "teacher's aid" in a taped-card machine if you can have one in your room. The programs I have seen are not geared for your children. However, if you do as I have, you can make some very imaginative programs that your children will love and learn a great deal from. I use blank tape-cards and cut them to get maximum use. After all if you are only recording single words you do not need four or more seconds of tape. I have also made my own cards from 3″ x 5″ index cards by gluing ordinary recorder tape carefully and exactly ½ inch from the bottom of the card and recorded over six hundred such cards which my students use constantly. Since the machine has unlimited time and patience at repeating hard-to-remember words and sounds, your children will never need to fear that it might be too tired to answer one more question at the end of a busy day and let even a little overtone of impatience creep into its voice.

CHAPTER 7

Letter Formation

The recipe for letter formation has many little ingredients. It may seem complicated at first, but as the saying goes, "inch by inch, it's a cinch." I wish I had discovered this method as a new teacher because it has been so successful in anticipating common pitfalls and putting in an ounce of prevention to avoid them.

Letter formation and recognition is vital to reading, of course. But children in school are often judged by their letter formation alone, when they are in a regular classroom or later when they go out to work, so extra attention paid to it at this very beginning stage will pay off for the child.

Form 26 letters from 12 jig-sawed figures.

If there is a wood shop at your school, ask the teacher if he can jig-saw some figures for

letters. I mention it now so that by the time you are ready to use them, he might have them ready for you.

RECIPE FOR MANUSCRIPT LETTERS

Ingredients:

For Teacher

Ditto Master of the Letter-Line figures, and the other figures in this chapter
Manila drawing paper 9″ x 12″
Black thin-point, felt-point pen
Large cut-out letter of black construction paper of each letter to put on your Letter Line
Large picture representing each beginning sound

For Children

Envelope for each child to hold his letter kit
Black crayon and one other color
Scissors
Ruled writing paper
Clay

Method:

1. Make enough copies of the following Letter Line figures stencil so you have at least two for each child and several extra for yourself. (One or two for the shop teacher, remember?)

2. Go over the lines with your thin-line black felt-point pen, including the face of the dragon on figure No. 2. I know this seems like extra work, but it will be worse if the children color the figure too heavily and can't see the ditto lines. Why not use colored paper? You'll see. It is one insurance against the reversal of this letter (c). Another insurance premium is the time it takes to go over the dragon face, but it will save so many reversals. You'll see!

LETTER LINE FIGURES

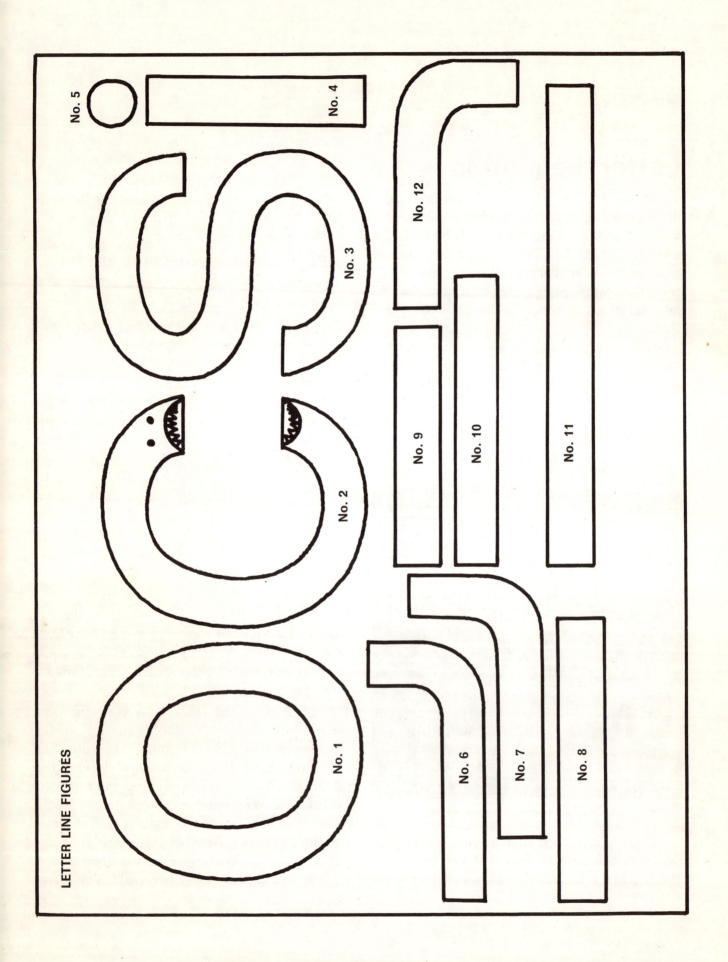

No. 5

No. 4

No. 1

No. 2

No. 3

No. 12

No. 9

No. 10

No. 11

No. 6

No. 7

No. 8

—c—

1. Cut out a block around shape No. 2 for each child. Ask him to look at it. Tell him the lines are in the shape of an "o" cookie that someone has taken a bite out of. It is the shape of the letter "c." Tell them this letter has the sound we hear at the beginning of words like *cat* and *cow*. Tell him that most "c" shapes do not have a dragon face on them, but this is a help on this one to learn this letter well.

2. Have the children color the whole block, but lightly so the lines will still show.

3. Ask them to trace over the lines with a black crayon (not the dragon's face) then cut along the black lines of the "c."

4. Tell them that if they turn it over to the uncolored side it is NOT a "c." This is the most important point of this lesson and is the reason for not using colored paper to begin with.

5. Show the children the large "c" you have cut from black construction paper and let them see you paste it on your Letter Line. Paste a large simple picture of a cat above it, as you remind them that the sound of "c" is heard at the beginning of this word.

6. The letters they have cut out should now lay on their desks, with the bite facing the same direction as the one you put on your Letter Line. If the bite is not in this direction the dragon is standing on his head. You'd better check each one to see that the opening is on the right side.

7. Have the children raise their right hands. If it helps, tell them it's the hand they use to salute the flag each morning. Check to be sure they have their *right* hands raised.

8. Now comes pretend: tell them the "c's" have their dragon mouths open, and by laying the first finger of their *right* hands in the opening, the dragon can "bite" that finger. That is the test to be sure the opening of "c" is on the correct side.

A group of reversal-prone letters depend on this first step.

9. Pass out paper now and give a brief writing lesson for "c" and let the children practice making it, being sure the dragon's mouth is ready to bite their right forefingers.

—a—

1. Make this a clay lesson for review of the pencil-sized straight line shape. Then show the children how to curve the pencil shape into a "c." Have them, with your help, test for the mouth of the "c." Ask them to lay the "c" aside for a minute.

2. Tell them: With a small piece of clay, make a crayon-sized straight line. Lay this short line alongside the open-mouth side of the "c" and a new letter, "a" is formed.

3. Show them the large black "a" you have cut from construction paper and paste it on your Letter Line.

4. Point out that one sound of the letter "a" is its name, and we hear it at the beginning of "apron." Maybe the children have never seen an apron, so be sure to have one handy to demonstrate it. Let anyone who wants to try it on. Paste a picture of an apron above the "a" on your letter line.

5. Let the children make whatever other figures they want to make with the clay for a while. When it is put away, give them figure No. 8 from the Letter Line figures to color the same color they made their "c" and trace the black line with a black crayon, then cut out this shape and lay it on their "c" shape, covering the mouth of the "c" and they will probably respond excitedly that they have made an "a."

6. Have a writing lesson on "a." Then have a writing review of i, l, o, c.

—d—

Now comes the letter that really triggered this whole sequence. If the direction of "c" and its open mouth have been stressed enough, *you* deserve a raisin or a cracker or a very large marshmallow because you have eliminated one of the biggest pitfalls for beginning readers! You are ready to teach a letter that is "d" and can be nothing else as long as it is started with a proper "c."

1. Give the children shape No. 11 to color and cut as they did before.

2. Have them take out their "c" shape; lay No. 11 on the "c" with the bottom of the No. 11 shape starting at the bottom of the "c."

3. Show them your large "d"; place it on your Letter Line; tell them it says the sound we hear at the beginning of "dog"; paste your picture of a dog above it.

4. Give a writing lesson on "d."

5. Use clay to reinforce the lesson if you wish. To add variety there is always the sand table where pictures of dogs and pictures of "d" may be traced in the slightly dampened sand; or some of the children may write on the chalkboard, or trace the sandpaper letters of i, l, o, a, d, that you have cut out and mounted.

— q —

Using the same two shapes: No. 2, No. 11, go through the above steps to form "q," the letter that sounds like the beginning of "queen." The only difference between "d" and "q" is that the No. 11 shape is even with the top of the "c" and extends below the "c" shape. The picture, of course, is of a queen.

— g —

Use shapes No. 2 and No. 11 to form a "q," then add shape No. 12 to curve the stem of the "q" and form a manuscript "g."

Note: "g" and "a" as seen in printed material have a slightly different form than the manuscript letters. This is not usually confusing to the children you are working with, but at some time during their early use of books, even if only for "reading" the pictures, you should tell them that sometimes these letters

are printed slightly differently, but the way they are being taught is the easiest way, and in any event they are learning the only way these letters will be written by them until we get to the capital letters.

Use the same procedure for teaching "g" as for the other letters outlined. The picture clue for "g" may be girl, and you should teach that this letter sounds like the sound we hear at the beginning of "girl."

— e —

Use shapes No. 2 and No. 4 to make "e," which is the sound of "e" we hear at the beginning of eagle, which is the picture clue for "e."

REVIEW OF THE FIRST BATCH OF LETTERS FROM RECIPE FOR MANUSCRIPT LETTERS

For this review, make a ditto stencil of the next illustration. Children will want to color the letters and pictures before they cut them out. If they color and cut one letter and its picture at a time, there will be little chance of mixing them up. Have them cut out the "i" and the iron and paste them back to back, then go on to the next letter and its picture. Emphasize that the picture word begins with the sound the letter makes in a word.

When all the letters and pictures are cut out and pasted, they may practice by placing the cards picture-side up on their tables and saying the picture words. As they say them have them also think and say the letter at the beginning of the word, and then turn the card over to check and see if they have said the correct letter. The cards they say correctly can go on one side of their desks while they work in the same way with the other cards, until they can say all the letters in connection with the pictures.

The group is now ready to suggest other words which begin with the same sound as the ones they have studied. Point to one of the pictures on your Letter Line. Say the beginning sound: "c" cat. See if anyone can say another word that begins with the sound. If they can't, have pictures of cow, candy, corn, cone, handy from your picture file. (Color books are great to use for simple line-drawings. Your children will love to color them for you.)

Begin a classification of "c" words and pictures somewhere on a wall in your room. If the wall space is completely used up already, hang a clothes line and pin pictures and words to it. If the pictures move, so much the better, they attract attention that way. Encourage them to bring pictures from home for each beginning sound.

This is a good time to start boxes of beginning sound objects: a box of objects beginning with the long sound of "i," the sound of "l," and the others. For "c" objects (pictures, too) use only those that have the hard "c" sound now to avoid confusion. In the same way, use only the long sound of "i" and "o."

By now, if you're lucky the shop teacher will have jig-saw shapes ready for you. If you are very lucky, he has made enough sets so each child has one in a box at his desk. Of course, you have painted or felt-point-penned the numbers on each shape so you can give each child only the numbers you have used in the Letter Formation Recipe so far. Give him a box to keep his shapes in at his desk so he can take them out to work with at any time. It is a fun activity to form the letters they know with these wooden shapes—good tactile learning, too.

Do be sure to point out (or help them point out) letters in their names that they have learned. The most important use of letters to these children is not that they unlock words for them, but that they appear in their own names.

With extra copies of the letter-picture page you ran off, glue letters to a cube (individual milk cartons painted with the canned-milk paint or enamel, or covered with contact paper make good cubes for this). Keep these cubes in a box on the game table. The object is to turn the cubes until the letter on one cube matches the picture on the other cube. Add other pictures beginning with these sounds. But . . .

Before putting *any* new game on the game table for independent use, be sure you have shown its use to *all* the children, so the important educational goal you had in mind in making the game is accomplished by its use.

CHAPTER 8

More Letter Formation

For a review of the letters in the last chapter and a springboard for the next group of letters, we have:

RECIPE FOR CHILDREN'S LETTER LINE
Ingredients:

For Teacher

Manila drawing paper, 12″ x 18″, one for each child

Ruler

Black thin-point, felt-point pen

For Children

Crayon

Scratch paper

Method:

1. Rule each 12″ x 18″ sheet like the following figure with the broken-line letters in the spaces.

2. Print each child's name on the back of his Letter Line, and hand them to the children.

3. Have the children recall the "i" shape, and practice it on scratch paper.

4. Direct them to find the broken-line figure of "i" on the Letter Line and trace it on the Letter Line with a crayon.

5. Follow steps 3 and 4 with l, o, c, e, a, d, g, q.

After the Letter Lines have been collected, go ahead with the same steps you used to teach each of the letters in the previous chapter. Use the shape numbers and key words listed here for the next set of letters.

— t —
Shapes No. 11 and No. 4
Key word—turtle

— h —
Shapes No. 11 and No. 7
Key word—hat

— k —
Shapes No. 11, No. 4, No. 9
Key word—kite

— f —
Shapes No. 11, No. 4, No. 12
Key word—fox

Hand out the Letter Lines (and scratch paper) and let the children add these new letters to theirs. Your own Letter Line at the front of the room will, of course, show your large black letter and a picture for each of these new letters. Your classification of pictures and your object box for each letter will be rapidly growing.

If you have a child who is troubled by having "c" and "k" both use the same sound, tell him that in most words "c" borrows the sound of "k." Sometimes it borrows another letter, too. Assure him that he will learn later just when to let "c" borrow "k's" sound and when another. I refer to the rule which is too complex to explain to children at this stage: the one which has "c" sound like "k" before "a, o, u," and like "s" before "e, i, y."

You have now taught half of the alphabet and four of the five vowels, so the children can have their first chance to make words. You can help them make words such as:

dog, log, fog

cat, hat

kite

cake

gate

Write them on the chalkboard and identify them with pictures from your picture file.

a	b	c	d

i	j	k	l

q	r	s	t

y	z

e	f	g	h

m	n	o	p

u	v	w	x

LETTER LINE

Taking a giant step, let's teach the children some sight words using letters they know:

I) is easily recognized as a pencil shape with a short line at the top and bottom. Tell them that when they speak about themselves they use this word.

a) is a word all by itself, that we use a great deal, but when we use it as a word we usually call it "uh."

the) is made up of three letters they already know: two tall letters and one short letter. Call attention to the configuration.

of) "o" should sound like "uh" in this word and the "f" sounds like "v." The configuration will help in remembering the word.

to) sounds the same as the number but has a different meaning.

On the chalkboard show the shape of these words and tell them the words. Show them and tell them how they can go with other words:

the dog   a dog
the cat   a cat
I go
I get

Then write these four words on the chalkboard and read them *for* them and then *with* them:

I get the cake.

Tell them this is a sentence because it tells something that is happening. Show them the period at the end of the sentence. Explain that it is a very small circle we call a dot. Point out that every sentence has some shape at the end of it and usually it is a period.

Another sentence uses the word "go."

I go to get the dog.

Make a display chart of these words, with pictures where appropriate, and of the sentence, to hang in sight of the children and refer to it often at odd moments during the day. Do not try to teach too many words. A few will whet their appetites for words, but too many will discourage them.

If you want the children to copy these words and sentences, teach them about leaving one letter's space between the words.

MORE LETTERS
Use the same steps you used before for teaching these letters:

— v —
Shapes No. 10, No. 8
Key word—vase

— w —
Shapes No. 10, No. 8, No. 9, No. 4
Key word—wolf

— x —
Shapes No. 10, No. 8
Key word—x-ray

— r —
Shapes No. 10, No. 12
Key word—rabbit

— y —
Shapes No. 9, No. 11
Key word—yarn

— j —
Shapes No. 11, No. 12, No. 5
Key word—jar

Give out the Letter Lines and scratch paper, and have the children write the new letters on them.

Have your new page of picture-letter stencils ready and have them color, cut and paste them to add to their letter-picture collection.

Do remember to keep your beginning sounds categories, the milk-carton letter-picture blocks and the object boxes up-to-date.

MORE LETTERS
Let's finish the small-letter alphabet, using those by-now familiar steps:

— n —
Shapes No. 10, No. 7
Key word—nest

— m —

Shapes No. 10, No. 7, No. 6
Key word—mug

— s —

Shape No. 3
Key word—sun

— z —

Shapes No. 4, No. 8, No. 9
Key word—zebra

— u —

Shapes No. 6, No. 8
Key word—uniform

The use of Shape No. 1 in the next two letters is most important. It is a final insurance against the reversal trap which "b" and "d" can become if you are not careful. When, in spite of your careful teaching, this reversal demon rears its head, go back to the letter formation lesson of "d" as it grows out of "c" and reteach it.

— b —

Shapes No. 1, No. 11
Key word—boy

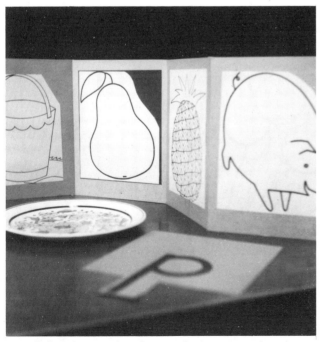

"p" is the sound we hear at the beginning of . . .

— p —

Shapes No. 1, No. 11
Key word—pumpkin

This is a time for you to become very dramatic:

Teach the word "can." Write the letters on the chalkboard. Have the children who can do so identify each letter as you write it. Show them the flat configuration pattern to help them remember the word. Explain that this is a picture word if they think of a can that holds food, and that it has another meaning like in "I can run."

Add the word "I" which is a memory word from the last lesson on words.

Teach a new word: "read." Tell them it says: (rēd).

Put the words:

I can read

together in large letters and see if anyone can tell you the words; or you may read it aloud to them. This is your big moment, and theirs. They have always known that they could not read, and now you are telling them they can.

Remind them of the chart on the wall that they have been "reading" and of the words they read during the earlier lesson on words. Allow each child to read this new sentence. Tell them there is much more to learn in order to read as much as they want to, but that they have taken a giant step in reading now.

For a relaxing time, give out the individual Letter Lines and have the children get out their letter-picture cards. You would be very wise to have several sets of these made up by more capable children who might be in your class or in one of the other classes in your school, so that you can always have one to fill in with. Alice or Jim will be sure to have one or two missing from their sets, and your whole lesson can be spoiled by the frustration they will feel if you can't instantly give them a replacement.

The letter-picture cards will be in jumbled order. Have the children use them for matching the letter to the Letter-Line letters. When this is done, have them turn each card over and say the picture word and its beginning sound like this:

> a says ā in apron
>
> b says (b) in boy

and so on. They can do this individually or with a partner.

The next step will be to take off all the cards, mix them up and lay them picture-side up on the appropriate beginning letter. This is a *learning* experience, NOT a *testing* time, so let them turn the card over to be reminded of the letter as much as they need to. After many tries they will remember. It's like learning to use a new recipe yourself. Even though you think you know how much of each ingredient to use, it's more reassuring to look once more and be sure.

Although this activity is presented in the form of a game, with rewards for completion (or for a good try), it can become tedious if it is repeated too many times, especially if it seems hard to do. Remember rewards, but also remember *variety of activity* are key words for these children. They will be interested in coming back to an activity if they are not over-exposed to it.

So . . . for variety . . . make up some stencils for Bingo-type games. An easy way to set up a group of Bingo stencils (that will not all be repeats so everyone wins at once) follows.

Make two master ditto stencils as shown.

Run off at least one for each child of both stencils. This gives you enough for a group game and for extras for the game table. Laminate the ones for the game table, or cover them with plastic (clear) contact paper, or enclose in plastic envelopes.

On the pages you have run off, scatter the

NUMBER 1

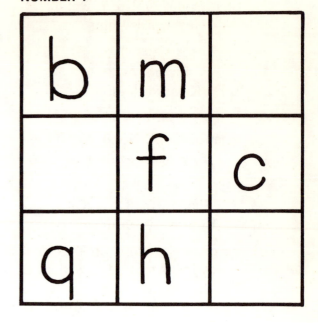

NUMBER 2

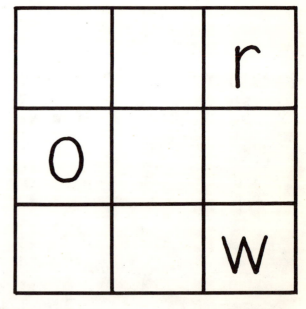

remaining letters of the alphabet at random. This way, each page will be different.

To play, use your large pictures from your file to hold before the group and have them place a button or a bean on the letter they hear at the beginning of the picture word.

64

You may use the same key words and duplicates of the pictures you have in your Letter Line since you are teaching not testing.

Use pictures that have the same subject as your Letter-Line pictures, but are not exact copies of them for a more advanced stage. Use other pictures of other objects for sound-letter identification for a still more advanced stage. The next step would be to use small objects instead of pictures thereby transferring the learning back to the concrete.

Use the game only as long as it remains exciting and fun, then put it away for another day.

Free Time! Let's make letters of clay.

CHAPTER 9

Capital Letters From Popsicle Sticks and Pipe Cleaners

Popsicle sticks are excellent helps to teach fifteen of the capital letters. You can buy 100 sticks for about 29c at a paper goods store. Or, you might prefer to start a collection of used ones (you can always dip them in alcohol to sterilize them) preparatory to this set of lessons. This is a good way to build enthusiasm. Many school cafeterias serve orange juice bars on popsicle sticks. Here is a built-in opportunity for cooperation between members of your class and the other children of the school. As with the milk carton blocks, the children not in your class will become curious about what the sticks are being used for, and wonder about the exciting things members of your class get to do. I have had children say, "I wish I could be in your class; your 'kids' have so much fun." You will get many more sticks than you will need for the capital letter lessons. Do be sure your children know that some of the uses for them will be to "dress" them as stick figures to represent characters in their favorite stories. They make wonderful stick puppets. Remember how proud you were when little timid Agatha let her voice ring out as the wicked step-mother in your puppet play of Cinderella? The stick figures may also be dressed and pasted to paper backgrounds for scenes from stories or real life, or used as characters in a shoe-box diorama.

A sharp knife will cut through the popsicle sticks for the half-sized pieces you will need to form the letters.

RECIPE FOR POPSICLE STICK
CAPITAL LETTERS
I, L, T, F, E, H

Ingredients:

For Teacher

One "baggie" for each child

Eleven popsicle sticks for each child, cut as follows:

    7 long

    6 halves

    4 quarters

Background paper for your Capital Letter Line below the Small Letter Line

Large black construction paper letters for the Capital Letter Line

For Children

Baggies filled as above

Crayons

Lined writing paper

Method:

— I —

We are starting with a familiar figure which the children already know as a word. Have them build the letter with a long stick and two quarter-size sticks as the cross bars. As you reteach "I" tell them that adding the cross bars is the only change. Associate the figure with the small "i," and let the children see you place your black paper I on your Capital Letter Line. Tell them it has the same sound as the small letter in words.

— L —

Have them build this letter from a long stick and a half stick. Identify your cut-out of it with the small "l" as you place it on your Capital Letter Line. Tell them it has the same sound the small "l" says.

— T —

One long stick and one half stick. Point out that a capital T has the cross bar at the top of the long stick and that the small "t" had the cross bar part way down from the top.

— F —

One long stick, one half stick, one quarter stick.

— E —

One long stick, two half sticks, one quarter stick. This letter may be built just after F has been made to point out the similarity between the two. There has been no confusion between these letters in my experience.

— H —

Two long sticks, one half stick.

Do stop after this first six letters and have a writing lesson on lined paper. Tell the children that all capital letters are tall and go from the top line to the bottom line.

Some of your children will recognize some of the capital letters, so you will have to be the judge of how fast to present them. Probably Tommy will recognize that T is the first letter of his name. Let him have his place in the sun for this, but tell the others that soon they will all have learned the first letter of their names.

The remaining nine stick letters fit into sets of three:

— V, W, X —

This is the easiest set.

— N, M, K —

These are a little more difficult and need careful writing practice.

A and Y are both difficult and need much careful writing practice.

Z should be easy as it is shaped just like the small "z."

You are half way through the Capital Letters, so if you make a Capital Letter Line for each child he can use his picture-letter cards to place the matching small letter on the Capital Letters you have taught him so far. Then, he can turn the cards over to the picture side and begin to connect the sounds of these new letter forms to the beginning sounds of the picture words.

Use clay to let the children form these new letters, and use the sand table for tracing them as you did with the small letters.

With a few boxes of "baggies" we can add a new practice activity.

RECIPE FOR BAGGIE LETTERS

Ingredients:

For Teacher

2 boxes of baggies
4 stencils
drawing paper 9″ x 12″
time
patience

For Children

crayons
cotton balls for erasers
writing paper

Method:

1. Prepare stencils with broken-line letters as in the following figure.

2. Run off the stencils onto the drawing paper. Cut the figures to 6″ x 6″. Put them in a baggie back-to-back. You will only need half as many as the number of children you have.

3. Give half the children one baggie and half the other. They will trace over the letters with crayon and copy them on their writing paper as many times as they can until you ring a bell for a signal to erase the crayoned

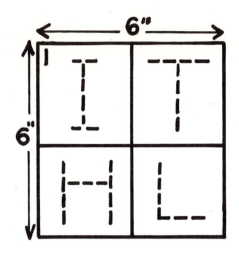

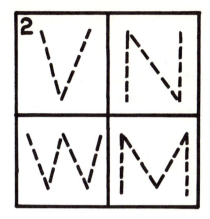

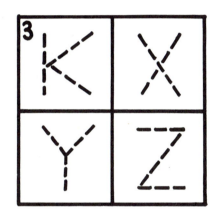

letters with the cotton ball and trade baggies with their neighbor.

As most of the games will, this will end up in a box on the game table for individual use.

The second half of the Capital Letter Alphabet uses the wide fuzzy pipe cleaners that come from school supply stores or hobby shops. Continue putting your large letters on your Capital Letter Line as each letter is presented, and give a writing lesson after each group of letters.

The first group has the letters based on a circle:

— O —

This is the easiest letter because it is the same as small "o."

— C —

An easy letter because it is like small "c."

— Q —

Like O with a small line added.

— G —

Like C with a small line added.
The next group includes:

— J —

Like a small "j" without the dot.

— P —

Like the small "p" but it stands on the writing line.

— R —

Like capital P but has a leg to stand on.
The last group of capitals includes:

— S —

Like a small "s" but larger.

— D —

A long straight line and a half circle.

69

— U —

Almost a horseshoe, but with straight sides.

— B —

Show them the figure 3 by drawing it on the chalkboard. Show them that when you put a line down before the openings in the 3 it is a perfect capital B. They can always check B by looking for the 3. When we write it, we put the straight line first and make the 3 so that its openings are closed by the line.

Do make a new set of baggie letters for these capitals, using the basic idea used in the Baggie Recipe.

Do use the children's Letter Line to further reinforce these new capitals and the sounds they have at the beginning of words.

Do use clay for making these new letters.

Then get ready for fun and NAMES.

As a celebration for learning all the letters it would be fun to give out a large sheet of paper and a scoop of miniature marshmallows and some paste to each child. They can make their own names out of the marshmallows that are not eaten. Since this is a food activity, a reward for finishing each name could be a free choice activity period for ten or fifteen minutes and a star beside each one's name on his attendance name card. If you do not have an attendance chart yet, here is a very simple one. The children move their names from "Out" to "In" each morning and put them in the "Out" column when they go home. It can be made more elaborate with the month, date and day and used as a reward for some child who gets to change these, or it can be your "reward" to do so.

Use a sheet of tagboard with tagboard name cards.

The milk carton blocks should now be complete with both small and capital letters so names may be built out of them. Teach them the fact that a capital letter is used to start their name and small letters for the rest.

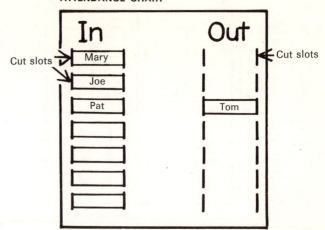

If you want to save your baggie letters to use next year, run off another set of stencils and insert them in more baggies, then cut them into blocks around the letters (into fourths), staple them to hold the baggie to them, and keep these in a handy box for building names.

Do teach them that the capital letter for their first name and for their last are their initials and are sometimes used instead of names.

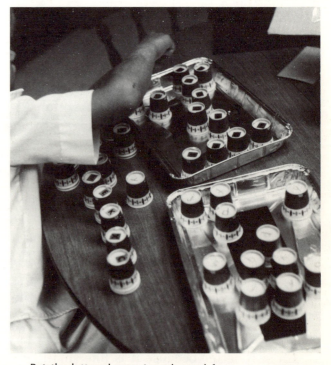

Put the lettered cups in order and form your name.

A game of matching small and capital letters as pairs is fun. Use the extra picture-letter cards you have made for yourself or for the game table. Lay the set of capital cards with them. Spread them all letter-side up on the table. Each person gets a turn to pick a letter and match it. If he can't find the matching letter, show it to him and let him find it next time it is his turn.

For a little harder game, give each player four cards and put four face up on the table with the rest in a stack in the center of the table. Each person in turn may either pick up one of the cards from the table to form a pair to lay beside him on the table, or if he can't find a match for any in his hand he may take one from the stack. The person with the greatest number of pairs at the end of the game is the winner.

Cut some 3″ x 5″ cards in two with variously shaped cuts. Colored cards are more interesting. Put a capital letter on one half and the matching small letter on the other half. Keep these in a small box on the game table.

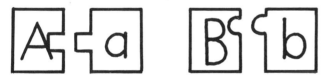

Let the children paste alphabet soup letters into names. Cereal letters that may be eaten are even better.

Make picture Bingo cards and have the children see if they can place the correct letter for the beginning sound over the picture. Start with pictures of the sounds that you have used for their Letter Lines. If you make

a stencil of these, the cards you give the children may all be alike and the game played as a group so everybody wins. You may graduate the difficulty by making stencils of other pictures, but still let everybody win for a while. Later you may mix the stencil pictures so only one or two win at a time. Using the basic stencil pattern I gave you for Letter Bingo, substituting pictures for the letters, will save you much time.

A race between two teams helps the children let off a little steam and learn at the same time. The teacher calls a letter and a member from each team goes to the chalkboard and writes it. The next person erases that letter and writes the next letter called. There is no need to have either team "win." This is an "everyone wins" game.

The woodshop teacher is probably interested in your projects by now and will make some letter shapes with his jig-saw for you. If he adds a little frame of a piece of plywood with a molding glued to it, the children can feel the letter shapes, getting the tactile experience they need to know them well, and can put them together into words on the frame.

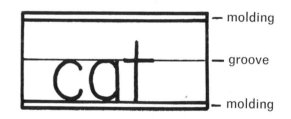

Use a combination of sticks and pipe cleaners to finish the Number Line lessons, basing your lessons on the procedure we used for letter formation.

CHAPTER 10

More Sensory and Motor Development

Johnny and Jane need to develop physical coordination before and during all other activities involved in reading preparation. Games that will develop their motor skills are, of course, part of your daily program, so I will add only a few others I have found helpful.

Do have an obstacle course now and then in your room. Lay it out with turned over chairs to go around or climb over, waste baskets or boxes to step in, a table to crawl under, large boxes to climb over and anything else you can put your hands on. Put these things into a pattern around the room, marked off with cotton roving string, if you wish. Have a goal at the end over and above the fun the children will have. They won't be aware of the balance and agility they are developing, but you will.

The hand-clapping game of Peas, Porridge Hot goes like this, in case you have forgotten it:

Peas, porridge hot

Hands touch thighs; hands clap together, hands clap partner's hands.

Peas, porridge cold

Repeat

Peas, porridge

Hands touch thighs, hands together.

In the pot

Right hand touches partner's right hand, hands together.

Nine days old.

Left hand touches partner's left hand, hands together, both hands touch partner's hands.

Some like it hot

Repeat the hand pattern to the rhythm of the second verse.

Some like it cold

Some like it

In the pot

Nine days old.

A pantomime of One, Two, Buckle My Shoe, makes exercise less tedious. In this one, only go as far as ten.

> One, two, buckle my shoe
> Three, four, shut the door
> Five, six, pick up sticks,
> Seven, eight, lay them straight
> Nine, ten, a big fat hen.

Don't overlook the jumping fun in:
> Jack be nimble, Jack be quick,
> Jack, jump over the candlestick.

My own game of Alphabet Jumping Jacks and Jills can be used with many variations. Even children who have "graduated" from

Hop the Alphabet Footsteps.

my classes come back to try it. I cut out twenty-six paper footprints (traced from a child's shoe), then print a lower-case 3″ letter on each. I lay them out in a walking pattern across the classroom floor. Contact paper cut with a one-inch border around the footsteps holds them to the floor and protects them.

Jacks and Jills walk around on the footsteps first, then go around them saying each letter they step on. After Jack has done this for a while and has learned to hop on one foot, he may hop on his preferred foot to "m" and on the other foot to "z." For variation, you may want the children to cross-pattern walk after they have learned to do this. (Walk normally, except pointing to the "walking" foot with the opposite hand, and alternating.) This is rather difficult and takes a good deal of practice, but is a very helpful coordination activity.

After a time, you might cut out another series of footsteps in another color. Put the capital letters on these and lay them down with a contact paper protection. They may start from a different section and bisect the small-letter footprint line.

The day Augustine was able to say all the letters, his brown eyes sparkled as he shouted, "I said them all!" That was all that he cared about, but I was delighted with his increased control of bodily movements, greater awareness of direction, and improvement in hand and eye muscle control.

Add to your children's hand and eye coordination in as many ways as you can. Make a box of objects and put a pair of kitchen tongs in it. Challenge the children to see what objects they can pick up with the tongs.

The tactile sense has been involved in most of the activities I have suggested, but there are so many more, you can let your imagination run wild.

Be sure you have many boxes of tactile games on your game table. Here are a few suggestions:

wooden beads of different shapes and colors to sort and to string

buttons of all shapes, sizes and textures

screws and bolts to sort and fit together

zippers to open and close

buttons and buttonholes—stitch the button and buttonhole part of a worn-out sweater or shirt together at top and bottom and you have a perfect manipulation game

cards with holes punched in the sides for lacing

an old boot to lace

Cross-pattern walking.

74

boxes of ribbon scraps to sort by color and texture

yarn scraps to sort by color and size

scraps of different textured material just to feel

small objects to sort and categorize—you can buy a bag of assorted plastic figures containing over a hundred for about a dollar

dolls to dress and undress

pop beads

Lincoln logs

Be sure you have a Feelie box of a variety of materials:

cloth, paper, cellophane, plastic, glass, rubber, sandpaper, fur, metal, wood.

These are interesting just for the tactile experience, and may be sorted as to hard and soft, rough and smooth. Make a Touch Board of some of them by mounting a square of different ones on cardboard.

Make a Mystery Feelie Box. Cut an arm opening in a box. Put various objects in it and seal the cover shut. Be sure the children are familiar with the objects you put into it. The child can reach in and with his eyes closed take out an object and try to tell what it is.

Or, you may ask the child to pick out the ball, or the paper clip.

Don't forget smell and taste are senses that need educating. Take some cotton balls and put some different smelling liquids on them: vanilla, almond extract, lemon juice, cologne, onion juice, coffee, even some dry spices like cinnamon or cloves. Identify them for the children, then play a guessing game to see if they can recall the smells. Use only two or three at one time.

Have a food-tasting time every few weeks. Try to have them guess the taste of familiar foods. Then add a few foods that the majority have never tasted. You may have to build up their interest in experimenting with new foods, but think how you are broadening their horizons. You might show pictures of places where the foods came from originally and tell a fact or two of interest about them. Have them look for likenesses and differences in how the following foods look and feel: sugar, salt, rice, flour, coffee beans, tea leaves, dry beans, popcorn.

Have fun with your children as you explore the world of sensory perception. Having fun while learning is what makes their whole school experience worthwhile.

CHAPTER 11

A Final Word: Love

No method that does not have love as its basis can be effective in the classroom. And the essential point in my method is love. All children need love, but the slow learner needs it more. Love and patience: this must be our last and most important recipe, and patience itself is a form of love.

You cannot expect standard responses and progress in your class, no matter what method you use. There are always individual variations, and these variations add to the joy of teaching these children. You discover more things about them, and about yourself, and about human nature.

Good teaching is not so much a matter of knowledge and experience as of being: an inner grace. There is a feeling of reverence for something sacred when we meet our obligations to these children and try to reach their unfolding minds through their hearts. Some of these hearts have been bruised before they come to us, and all require tender care. You have to be gentle with them. They feel insecure. You cannot force knowledge on any child. What the child learns will stay longer with him if you make it fun, a playful activity.

The gates of heaven are said to be open to children, and there is a bit of heaven around us when we are with children. I like to think the gates are open a little wider to those who learn to read more slowly. There are no "retarded" children in God's eyes. They are like other children, only more childlike perhaps, little individuals whose childhood is prolonged, and teaching them has its own wonders, rewards, and blessings.

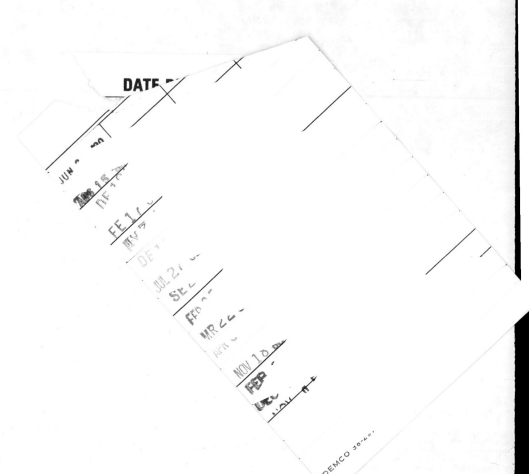

DATE

JUN

DEMCO